INTERNATIONAL LAW AFLOAT ON A SEA OF WORLD RELIGIONS

INTERNATIONAL LAW AFLOAT ON A SEA OF WORLD RELIGIONS

Religion and Law Series, Volume Five

George J. Gatgounis

WIPF & STOCK · Eugene, Oregon

INTERNATIONAL LAW AFLOAT ON A SEA OF WORLD RELIGIONS

Religion and Law Series, Volume Five

Copyright © 2022 George J. Gatgounis. All rights reserved. Except for brief quotations in critical publications or reviews, no part of this book may be reproduced in any manner without prior written permission from the publisher. Write: Permissions, Wipf and Stock Publishers, 199 W. 8th Ave., Suite 3, Eugene, OR 97401.

Wipf & Stock
An Imprint of Wipf and Stock Publishers
199 W. 8th Ave., Suite 3
Eugene, OR 97401

www.wipfandstock.com

PAPERBACK ISBN: 978-1-7252-6128-0
HARDCOVER ISBN: 978-1-7252-6129-7
EBOOK ISBN: 978-1-7252-6130-3

VERSION NUMBER 031822

CONTENTS

INTERNATIONAL LAW AFLOAT
ON A SEA OF RELIGION ETHICS | 1

RELIGIONS AS WORLDVIEWS | 3

WORLDVIEWS AS SOURCES OF LAW | 4

GENERAL PRINCIPLES COMMON
TO EACH RELIGION EXAMINED | 5
   One International Deity | 5
   One International Community | 6
   One International Creator | 6
   Relations between Humankind on the Personal,
      Collective, and International Levels | 7
   The Golden Rule as a Social and International Ethic | 8
   The Principle of Social and International Peace | 10
   Giving Enjoined in Social and International Contexts | 10
   The Principle of Truth-Telling in Social
      and International Contexts | 11

CONFUCIAN INFLUENCE ON THE DEVELOPMENT
OF INTERNATIONAL LAW | 13
   Confucianism's International Goal | 13
     The Great Harmony: The Goal of Confucianism | 13
     The Great Way: The Means of Achieving
       the Great Harmony | 15
   Confucianism's Conception of World Community | 16

 The State of the World Community in Confucius' Time | 16
 The Reformation of the World Community
  in Confucius' Time | 17
Confucianism's Conception of World Order | 18
 Ethics over Law | 18

HINDU INFLUENCE ON THE DEVELOPMENT OF INTERNATIONAL LAW | 20

 The Hindu Law of Maintaining Interstate Peace | 21
 The Hindu Law of War | 22
  Ethical Limitations | 24
 The Hindu Law of Neutrality | 25

THE CHRISTIAN INFLUENCE ON THE DEVELOPMENT OF INTERNATIONAL LAW | 27

 The Foundational Contribution of Grotius | 27
  Grotius' Purpose in Writing *De Jure Belli Ac Pacis* | 27
  Grotius on International Relations between "Christian"
   and "Pagan" Nations | 32

THE INFLUENCE OF ISLAM ON THE DEVELOPMENT OF INTERNATIONAL LAW | 34

 The Quran as a Source of Law and Government | 34
  Quranic Law | 34
  The Quran's Doctrine of Government of Allah | 35
  The Quran's Prescriptions on the Relation of Islamic Nations
   with Non-Islamic Nations | 36
  The Quranic Doctrine of "Mosque" and "State" | 38
  Increasing Secularization under the Realities of Statecraft
   over Conquered Peoples | 39
  Islamic Poetry—A Reflection of the Islamic View
   of International Relations | 40
  The Islamic Doctrine of Holy War or J'had | 44
  The Nebulous Nature of Islamic Political Thought | 45
  The Development of an Islamic Orthodoxy | 45
  Islamic Law and International Law | 46
  The Practical Problems of Imposition of Islamic Law
   upon Nations | 47

Methodological Considerations in Evaluating the Ramifications
    of Islamic Resurgence to International Law | 49
Spheres of Islamic Political Activism | 50
  The Eradication of Western-Imported Legal Systems
      and the Reinstitution of Islamic Law | 50
  Increased Religious Allusion and Symbolism | 51
  Metamorphosis of Social Mores | 52
  Political Activist Organizations | 53
  International Organizations to Promote Unity
      among Islamic Nations | 54
  Educational Reform | 55
The Delicate Balance Moderate Arab States Must Follow
    in Foreign Policy | 55
A Focus on Shiite Activism | 56
A Focus on the Role of Islamic Resurgence in the Foreign
    Policy of Qadhdafi | 57
  The General Pattern of Erosion of *Sharica* and Absorption
      of Western Legal Codes | 57
  Qadhdafi's Role of Limiting the *Sharica* in Libya | 59
  Qadhdafi's Redefinition of the Divine Law, the *Sharica* | 59
  Qadhdafi's Attack on Islamic Shirk or Para-Quranic
      Religious Documents | 60
  Qadhdafi's Standing with Shiite Revolutionaries | 61
A Focus on the Iranian Revolution and Its Doctrine
    of International Expansion | 62
  Islam as a Catalyst for International Revolution | 62
  The International Ramifications of the Rise
      of Ayatollah Khomeini | 63
  Militant Shia Fueling War with Iraq | 64
  National Statutes Resulting from the Shiite Revolution | 64
The Impact of the Constitution of the Islamic Republic
    upon International Law | 68
  The Pan-Islamic Component of the Iranian Constitution | 68
International Response to the Iranian Revolution | 69
  The Formation of the Gulf Cooperation Council | 69

CONCLUSION | 71
BIBLIOGRAPHY | 73

INTERNATIONAL LAW AFLOAT ON A SEA OF RELIGION ETHICS

Of the many books that have been written concerning the various areas of law, comparatively few are focused on international law, and even less on the ethical basis for international law. Popular thinking has developed a reasonable explanation for this omission, alleging that since there is no highest world court or legislature legally binding all the nations, international law, technically, does not exist. For law to be law, the law must be enforceable. There is no governing legislature or judiciary with a world police force.

This is a valid theory, of course, but issues of any real importance to human existence do not stay in the theoretical realm—for an issue to have relevance, it must have roots that are firmly planted in human experience. Human experience regarding international law is such that when confronted by acts of depravity on the part of a national government, an unofficial world court arises to offer judgment and non-existent laws grow "teeth," meaning world opinion, trade sanctions, international isolation, and military containment or conflict.

This work is striking in its boldness. Through writing it, Dr. George Gatgounis extracts himself from the serenity and comfort of mere theory to join us in the complicated and dangerous world in which we all reside. The depth of Dr. Gatgounis' knowledge is astonishing, but what truly separates him from his contemporaries is his common-sense practicality. This book is an admonition that ignoring the ethical base of international law may turn us to amoral pragmatists, driven by mere expediency.

"The Lord is high above all nations" (Psalm 113:4 ESV), and in accord with the propriety of that declaration, international law in the pre-17th-century Christian era derived from religious ethics. Dr. George Gatgounis, Esq. explores how religious ethics undergirded the development of international law, creating an ideal for the foundation for international conventions, customs, standards, and "laws."

H. Wayne House

RELIGIONS AS WORLDVIEWS

A particular state's body of law presupposes some kind of worldview. Some worldviews are religious in character. The following religions, Confucianism, Hinduism, Christianity, and Islam, have philosophical systems which bear upon the formation of law, including international law. Now is the time to explore, in at least in a cursory manner, the contributions of Confucianism, Hinduism, Christianity, and Islam to the development of international law. Each of these philosophical systems provides ideological underpinnings for both domestic and international law.

WORLDVIEWS AS SOURCES OF LAW

Worldviews are sources of law. The following worldviews explored have remarkable common ground. Various elements of these religions include some conception of deity, an ethic for interpersonal relations, and a vision for a world in conformity with their precepts. Each worldview, therefore, has as its ultimate goal the conversion of all nations to its principles. Each of the religions discussed promises world harmony, unity, and prosperity beyond what history has recorded if its tenets become personal, national, and international norms.

GENERAL PRINCIPLES COMMON TO EACH RELIGION EXAMINED

ONE INTERNATIONAL DEITY

Various religions, including Islam and Hinduism, espouse a conception of deity which is universal. As the following prayers of Islam and Hinduism reflect, deity here is truly international in lordship. One Islamic prayer reflecting the conception of an international Lord reads as follows:

> Praise be to God, the Lord of all
> creatures; the most merciful, the king of
> the day of judgment. Thee do we
> worship, and of thee do we beg
> assistance. Direct us in the right way, in
> the way of those to whom thou hast been
> gracious; not of those against whom thou
> art incensed, nor of those who go astray.[1]

Similarly, the following Hindu supplication reveals a concept of deity which is universal:

> Supreme Lord! Lord of warmth and light,
> Of life and consciousness, that knows all,
> Guide us by the right path to happiness,
> And give us strength and will to war against
> The sins that rage in us and lead us astray.

---

1. Jeffry Moses, *Oneness: Great Principles Shared by All Religions* (New York: Fawcett Columbine, 1989), p. 119.

We bow in reverence and prayer to Thee. Aum.[2]

ONE INTERNATIONAL COMMUNITY

Further, a variety of religious texts commend some form of unity of humankind. The Apostle Paul, for instance, in his speech to the Athenians in Acts 17, stated the common source of all humankind, the One Creator who "hath made of one blood all nations of men." Islam includes a similar articulation of the source of all peoples: "All creatures are the family of God; and he is the most beloved of God who does most good unto His family." Hinduism sees humankind as an organic social unity: "Human beings all are as head, arms, trunk, and legs unto one another." Moreover, Shintoism sees humankind as a singular family: "Do not forget that the world is one great family."[3]

ONE INTERNATIONAL CREATOR

Many religions view deity as creator. Both Christianity and Judaism see humankind as the product of the direct creative act of God. Genesis 1:28 states that God "created man in his own image, in the image of God created he them." Islam echoes the same principle: "God's own nature has been molded in man's." Sikhism takes the creation principle a step further and claims that God is in very soul and that the individual soul is part of a collective whole, a singular universal human soul.[4] Sikhism states, "God is concealed in every heart; his light is in every heart." Hinduism adds that the individual soul is nothing else in essence that universal soul."[5]

---

2. *Ibid.*, p. 119.
3. *Ibid.*, pp. 114–15.
4. *Ibid.*, pp. 110–11.
5. *Ibid.*

GENERAL PRINCIPLES COMMON TO EACH RELIGION EXAMINED

RELATIONS BETWEEN HUMANKIND ON THE PERSONAL, COLLECTIVE, AND INTERNATIONAL LEVELS

Love is a common note in the various theologies of the world's predominant religions. Buddhism includes a maxim remarkably like Jesus': "He that loveth not, knoweth not God. For God is love." Judaism's Talmud states similarly: "Love is the beginning and end of the Torah."[6] The Apostle Paul in Romans 13 stated that "love is the end of the law." "He that loveth another fulfilleth the law." Johannine theology parallels Pauline theology. First John 4:7 and 8 restate the Pauline maxim: "Beloved, love one another, for love is of God, and he that loveth another abideth in God, and God abideth in him."

Love is also a command of Confucianism: "Love belongs to the high nobility of heaven, and is the quiet home where man should dwell."[7] Sufism echoes the near universal love principle:

> Sane and insane, all are searching lovelorn
> For Him, in mosque, temple, church, alike.
> For only God is the One God of Love,
> And Love calls from all these, each one His home.[8]

In the Gospel of John, Jesus taught, "A new commandment I give unto you, That you love one another; even as I have loved you. By this shall all men will know that you are my disciples, if you have love for one another." Confucius similarly required that people should "seek to be in harmony with all your neighbors; live in amity with your brethren." Shintoism also requires: "Regard Heaven as your father, Earth as your mother, and all things as your brothers and sisters."[9] Buddha commanded: "Full of love for all

---

6. *Ibid.*, p. 106.
7. *Ibid.*, p. 106.
8. *Ibid.*, p. 107.
9. *Ibid.*, p. 31.

things in the world, practicing virtue in order to benefit others, this man alone is happy."[10]

THE GOLDEN RULE AS A SOCIAL AND INTERNATIONAL ETHIC

Both Moses and Jesus taught, "Thou shalt love thy neighbor as thyself." "Do you unto others as you would have them do unto you, for this is the law and the prophets" was the central command of Jesus regarding interpersonal relationships. Judaism's Talmud reiterates: "What is hurtful to yourself do not to your fellow man. That is the whole of the Torah and the remainder is but commentary."[11] Remarkably, Hinduism has virtually verbatim the same command: "A man obtains a proper rule of action by looking on his neighbor as himself."[12] Islam does not differ from Hinduism, Judaism, and Christianity in this ethic: "Do unto all men as you would wish to have done unto you: and reject for others what you would reject for yourselves."[13] Buddha taught, "Hurt not others with that which pains yourself." Confucius taught the same principle through the following dialogue:

> Tzu-Kung asked: "Is there one principle upon which one's whole life may proceed?" The Master replied, "Is not Reciprocity such a principle?—what you do not yourself desire, do not put before others."

Hinduism similarly states in the maxims:

> This is the sum of all true righteousness—
> Treat others, as thou wouldst thyself be treated.
> Do nothing to thy neighbor, which hereafter
> Thou wouldst not have thy neighbor do to thee.

---

10. *Ibid.*, p. 31.
11. *Ibid.*, p. 6.
12. *Ibid.*, p. 30.
13. *Ibid.*, p. 6.

GENERAL PRINCIPLES COMMON TO EACH RELIGION EXAMINED

The predominant religions commend love and condemn hatred. The Proverbs of both Judaistic and Christian Scriptures state: "He who is slow to anger has great understanding, but he who has a hasty temper exalts folly." Chapter four of the book of Ephesians in the New Testament states, "Let not the sun go down upon your wrath." Shintoism states the same: "Let us cease from wrath and refrain from angry gestures."[14] Similarly, Buddhism condemns anger: "He who holds back rising anger like a rolling chariot, him I call a real driver; others only hold the reins."[15]

The ethic of refraining from destructive acts plays heavily in the realm of international relations. Hinduism states: "Do not hurt others, do no one injury by thought or deed, utter no word of pain to thy fellow creatures." Buddhism holds similarly: "Hurt none by word or deed, be consistent in well-doing."[16] Jainism states, "Master of his senses and avoiding wrong, one should do no harm to any living being, neither by thoughts nor words nor acts."[17] So Islam holds in agreement: "Whatever good you do for others, you send it before your own soul and shall find it with God, who sees all you do."[18] Finally, the Apostle Paul agrees in his command to the Ephesians in chapter four, verse thirty two: "Be ye kind to one another, tenderhearted, forgiving one another, even as God for Christ's sake hath forgiven you."

According to this nearly universal religious ethic, nations are to treat each other as they themselves would want to be treated. Application of this principle encounters difficulty in arenas such as international espionage. Which nation would want its military capacity fully known by a potential aggressor? The Golden Rule applied to nations would rule out aggression, which is a fear, at least to some degree, of every nation.

---

14. *Ibid.*, p. 79.
15. *Ibid.*, p. 79.
16. *Ibid.*, p. 70.
17. *Ibid.*, p. 71.
18. *Ibid.*, p. 71.

THE PRINCIPLE OF SOCIAL AND INTERNATIONAL PEACE

Jesus' Beatitude in chapter five of the Book of Matthew is an immortal invocation to peacemaking: "Blessed are the peacemakers: for they shall be called the children of God." Islam also enjoins peacemaking: "Shall I tell you what acts are better than fasting, charity, and prayers? Making peace between enemies are such acts; for enmity and malice tear up the heavenly rewards by the roots."

Hinduism commends a similar ethic: "The noble-minded dedicate themselves to the promotion of peace and the happiness of others—even those who injure them."[19]

The same social ethic is repeated in Buddhism: "When righteousness is practiced to win peace, he who so walks shall gain the victory and all fetters utterly destroy."[20] The Christian and Hebrew Scripture in Isaiah chapter forty affirms the loveliness of those who proclaim peace: "How beautiful upon the mountains are the feet of him who brings good tidings, who publishes peace."[21]

GIVING ENJOINED IN SOCIAL AND INTERNATIONAL CONTEXTS

Christ, according to the Apostle Paul, declared, "It is more blessed to give than to receive." Taoism reiterates the same concept: "Extend your help without seeking reward. Give to others and do not regret or begrudge your liberality. Those who are thus are good."[22] Sikhism teaches similarly: "In the minds of the generous contentment is produced."[23] Islam holds "the poor, the orphan, the captive—feed them for the love of God alone, desiring no reward, nor even thanks."[24] Hinduism likewise commends to those with need:

19. *Ibid.*, p. 38.
20. *Ibid.*, p. 39.
21. *Ibid.*, p. 39.
22. *Ibid.*, p. 22.
23. *Ibid.*, p. 22.
24. *Ibid.*, p. 23.

"Bounteous is he who gives to the beggar who comes to him in want of food and feeble."[25]

THE PRINCIPLE OF TRUTH-TELLING IN SOCIAL AND INTERNATIONAL CONTEXTS

The Apostle Paul commanded the Ephesians in the fourth chapter of his letter as follows: "Putting away lying, speak every man truth with his neighbor: for we are members of one another." The Old Testament of Christianity, which composes the complete Hebrew Bible, states "speak ye every man truth to his neighbor, execute the judgment of truth and peace in your gates."[26] Buddha clearly regarded the truth teller as having desirable character: "Him I call indeed a Brahmana who utters true speech, instructive and free from harshness, so that he offends no one."[27] Islam requires truth telling also: "Do not clothe the truth with falsehood; do not knowingly conceal the truth."[28] Hinduism does not differ with Christianity, Judaism, Buddhism, and Islam in its command: "Say what is true! Do thy duty. Do not swerve from the truth." Confucius ably articulated the same principle:

> Sincerity is the way of Heaven, and to think how to be sincere is the way of a man. Never was there one possessed of complete sincerity who did not move others. Never was there one without sincerity who was able to move others.[29]

If this principle of truth telling became reality in the international arena, no nation would cheat upon its international treaties. Nazi Germany would never have invaded the Rhine without first formally abrogating the Treaty of Versailles. The now-defunct Soviet Union would not have violated stipulations of

25. *Ibid.*, p. 23.
26. *Ibid.*, p. 18.
27. *Ibid.*, p. 18.
28. *Ibid.*, p. 19.
29. *Ibid.*, p. 19.

the 1972 Anti-Ballistic Missile Treaty in developing ground-based anti-missile lasers and related anti-ballistic missile weaponry. This principle of international truth telling, however, could be circumvented by change of a nation's government. Nazi Germany, for instance, in violating the Treaty of Versailles, could claim, "It was not us who signed it. The Kaiser signed it, and therefore he alone, if in power, is honor bound to obey it. We are new government with no such obligations." Truth telling, however, if it became an international norm, would be a colossal step toward world peace.

CONFUCIAN INFLUENCE ON THE DEVELOPMENT OF INTERNATIONAL LAW

Confucianism lacks three of the most prominent common denominators of the religions of the world. Confucianism includes no belief in a deity or deities, no doctrine of salvation, and no doctrine of the afterlife.[1] Confucianism includes, however, rituals, a code of conduct, and doctrines of human nature, human values, and human institutions.[2] Regarding human government in a worldwide scope, Confucianism has an international goal, a conception of world community, and a conception of international order.[3]

CONFUCIANISM'S INTERNATIONAL GOAL

The Great Harmony: The Goal of Confucianism

Confucianism's goal for international relations is summarily comprehended in one word—*ping*,[4] which denotes "peace, harmony,

---

1. Mark W. Janis, ed. *The Influence of Religion on the Development of International Law* (Dordrecht: Martinus Nijhoff Publishers, 1991), p. 31.
2. *Ibid.*, p. 31.
3. *Ibid.*, p. 31.
4. *Ibid.*, p. 32; Ping is described in Confucius' magnum opus, *Great Learning*. *Great Learning* is actually four books, including *Great Learning, The Doctrine of the Mean, The Confucian Dialects,* and *The Works of Mencius.*

evenness, equality, and fairness."[5] When the "Great Way"[6] has overcome the entire world, the world has achieved the "Great Harmony."[7] The "Great Way" is an economic and social Golden Rule. Confucius saw the "Great Way" and "Harmony" as a utopian world community in the past.[8] In the past world utopia, Confucius, envisioned worldwide social equality. This world utopia was "equally shared by all."[9] Although marked by equality, the world utopia displayed great diversity. "Worthy and able" administrators "were chosen as office-holders."[10] "Good neighborliness" was so intense that adults treated all children as their own. Children treated all adults as if they were their own parents.[11] The aged, including widows and widowers, the orphaned, the sick, and the disabled received all the care they needed. Men served as bread winners and women served as keepers of their homes. Selfish motives did not exist in this world utopia. Although no one desired anything of wealth to be wasted, no one desired wealth because of greed. Thus, "robbers," "thieves," and "other lawless elements failed to arise." Even the doors of houses did not have to be locked.[12] The Confucian past vision of *ping* was economic prosperity in the context of a "peaceful and happy" social order.[13] The goal of the Confucian social ethic is restore the world to its original *ping*.

---

5. *Ibid.*, p. 32.

6. *Ibid.*

7. *Ibid.*; L.F. Chen, *The Confucian Way: A New and Systematic Study of the Four Books* (1977), p. 577.

8. *Ibid.*, p. 32.

9. *Ibid.*, p. 32.

10. *Ibid.*, p. 32.

11. *Ibid.*

12. *Ibid.*, p. 32.

13. *Ibid.*; James Legge, *The Chinese Classics* (Delhi: Motilal Banarsidass, 1966), I, p. 359.

The Great Way: The Means of Achieving the Great Harmony

The means to attain worldwide *ping* are the virtues of each individual. The *Book of Great Learning* includes the various virtues each member of the world community is to attain. The *Book of Great Learning* is the "gate by which first learners enter into virtue."[14] The *Book of Great Learning* describes seven pedestals to worldwide *ping*. First, each individual must develop the virtue of the investigation of things. Each learner must attain a mind set of objective analysis of all their surroundings. Second, each must extend their knowledge. Each learner must expand and fill the mind as much as possible with knowledge. Third, each must regulate their thoughts so that each thought is sincere. A thought life composed of sincere thoughts was a means to sincere character. Fourth, each must rectify their heart. Emotions and affections must be ordered so that one has good character. Fifth, each must cultivate himself or herself. Self-cultivation is the conscious development of one's character. Sixth, each must stand in a right relation with their family. Confucius saw the relation to one's family as extremely important to development of world harmony. Seventh, each must contribute to the proper government of the state.[15] When each world member once again attains each of these virtues, then the world will have the universal and utopian *ping*. The perfection of self necessarily precedes the perfection of the state. The first five virtues consist in perfecting self; the next three consist in the perfecting of groups.[16] Confucius summarized the hurdles that mankind overcame on the path to past worldwide *ping* in the *Book of Great Learning*:

> Things investigated, knowledge became complete; knowledge complete, thoughts were sincere; thoughts sincere, hearts were rectified; hearts rectified, persons were cultivated; persons cultivated, families were regulated; families regulated, states were rightly governed;

---

14. *Ibid.*, p. 32; James Legge, *The Chinese Classics* (Delhi: Motilal Banardiass, 1966).
15. *Ibid.*, p. 32.
16. Ibid, p. 35.

states rightly governed, the whole world was made tranquil and happy.[17]

To faithful Confucians, the "adjustment of the great invariable relations of mankind and the establishment of the great fundamental virtues of humanity" are paramount.[18] Confucians are to "treat all China as one person and all under heaven as one family."[19]

Confucius' principle of right ethics developed internally, then in families, then in nations, and then the entire world provides a challenging gauntlet. Confucius, like the consensus of contemporary sociologists, understood even in his ancient era, the building blocks of national order are healthy families. Confucius' order of developing socially acceptable behavior was first self, then family, then nation, then community of nations.

CONFUCIANISM'S CONCEPTION OF WORLD COMMUNITY

The State of the World Community in Confucius' Time

Confucius developed his conception of world community during 722–841 B.C., the "Spring and Autumn" era of Chinese history.[20] Confucius saw little, if any, requisites to world *ping* in this era. Mencius, an associate of Confucius, described the corruption of the time. "The world was fallen into decay, and right principles were dwindled away."[21] Even sons were murdering their fathers.[22] The King of eastern Chou, the ruler of the Chinese kingdom, had

---

17. *Ibid.*, p. 35; Confucius, *Great Learning* (China: Commercial Press, 1923), pp. 5–7.

18. *Ibid.*, p. 34; but Chen in this note states "I have lost the source from which I took these remarks." Compare *Analects* Book 12, Chapter 5.

19. *Ibid.*, p. 34; Chen adds that the *Analects* Book 12, Chapter 5 contain generally the utopian vision of worldwide Confucianism.

20. *Ibid.*, p. 33; see generally Mencius, *Work of Mencius* (New York: New American Library, 1960), Bk. III, pt. II, chapter 9.

21. *Ibid.*, p. 33; Mencius, *Work of Mencius*, Bk. III, pt. II, chapter 9.

22. *Ibid.*, p. 33.

little authority over the various provinces. Each province was a virtual independent state. To Confucius, the world consisted of "all under heaven" or *tien-hsia*. Although in some contexts Confucius used the term to describe the fragmented Chinese kingdom, some contexts imply a wider scope of meaning, the entire community of mankind. Confucius' worldview extended to the fragmented Chinese kingdom and those few border "barbarian" states surrounding it.[23] The seventh virtue in the *Book of Great Learning*, world government, was absent in Confucius' worldview in his era. Interstate friction within the so-called Chinese Empire of eastern Chou and border strife blemished any hope for world *ping*. *Tien-hsia* was dismal in Confucius' era.

The Reformation of the World Community in Confucius' Time

Confucius nurtured hope in the midst of despair. Because of the political impotence of the king of the fragmented Chinese Empire,[24] he realized that the "Great Way" could be implemented only through the authorities in the various provinces and border states. To implement the "Great Way," Confucius traveled to various provinces to seek public office. If he could gain influence over the local sovereign, he could teach that sovereign the "nine standard rules for the government of *tien-hsia* articulated in his book *The Doctrine of the Mean*.[25] This state could serve all other states as an "illustration of the illustrious virtue all under heaven."[26]

One of Confucius' rules was the "indulgent treatment of people from a distance."[27] Confucius argued that all people should be treated equally, even the so-called barbarians. Accordingly, Confucius taught in his book *Spring and Autumn* that righteousness

23. Ibid.
24. Ibid., p. 33.
25. Ibid; p. 34; *Doctrine of the Mean*, Chapter 32, volume 1.
26. Ibid., p. 35; Confucius, *Great Learning* (China: Commercial Press, 1923), p. 1.
27. Ibid; p. 34.

consisted of treating the Chinese as barbarians if they acted like barbarians and the barbarians as Chinese if they acted like Chinese.[28] If Confucius' teaching spread from one state to another within the Chinese Empire, barbarians within the Empire would hear and send word to the border states of the desirability of social equality. In a related vein, Mencius, the associate of Confucius, argued that the well-governed state could spread *ping* over the entire *tien-hsia* by expanding over all peoples. The necessity of "expansion" implies the necessity for diplomatically induced mergers and even war.

CONFUCIANISM'S CONCEPTION OF WORLD ORDER

Ethics over Law

The Chinese terms *li* and *fa* are key terms in the Confucian worldview that demonstrate the distinctiveness of the Confucian conception of world order. The Confucian views *fa* or law as a necessary evil. *Fa* is unpleasant. Society should be not regulated by *fa* externally applied upon each individual. Rather, society should be regulated by internal ethical principles in the minds of every citizen.[29] Personal ethics or *li* is higher moral ground that *fa*. *Li* accomplishes the same purpose as *fa* but only more effectively and elegantly.[30] Janis, the Confucian scholar, contends that the proposition that *li* is preferred over *fa* is an oversimplification. To Janis, *li* includes both law and morals. Janis concurs with Po-chi Wang, another Confucian scholar, that *li* is best translated "social norms."[31] The concept of "social norm" includes the concept of "juridical norm" because some social violations include criminal

---

28. Ibid; p. 34.

29. *Ibid.*, p. 35–36; Lord Lloyd of Hampstead, *Introduction to Jurisprudence* (London: Stevens, 1979), pp. 760–1.

30. *Ibid.*, p. 35–36.

31. *Ibid.*, p. 37.

sanctions.[32] Wrongdoing results in a "socially organized reaction" which includes an ethical response by those who disapprove and a legal response by sanctions. But clearly in the Confucian mind set, if ethics prevailed in every case, law would not be necessary.[33] If a "self-perfected" person should lapse into an unethical act, the person, out of a sense of shame, would voluntarily render to the one wronged their due.[34] Therefore, in the Confucian view, as virtue grows litigation decreases. In world *ping*, personal ethics will rule rather than adjudication.

---

32. *Ibid.*, p. 37.
33. *Ibid.*, p. 38.
34. *Ibid.*, p. 38.

HINDU INFLUENCE ON THE DEVELOPMENT OF INTERNATIONAL LAW

The Hindu contributions to the development of international law include principles for the maintaining of peace between states, principles guiding the waging of war between states, and principles regarding neutrality between nations. Ancient India, because of its decentralized network of nation-states, was a fertile environment for the development of international principles of war, neutrality, and peace. As early as the Rig Veda period (1,100 B.C.), the science of statecraft or *desadharma* developed. The central doctrine of *desadharma* was self-government by general rules of righteousness or *dharma*. During the Rig Veda period, nation-states were ruled as monarchies.[1] Monarchs were to rule according to the rules of *dharma* as found in religious works called *Sruti, Dharmasutstras, Smritis, Epics,* and *Puranas,* and secular works such as Kautily's *Arthasastra* or the *Science of Ways and Means.*[2] These rules of *dharma* applied regardless of the size of the nation-state, its religion, the race or races composing it, and whether any particular war which the nation-state waged was just or unjust.[3] In this period, personal, social, domestic, and international norms

---

1. Ibid., p. 51; S. Viswanatha, *International Law in Ancient India* 10, (1929), pp. 6–7.

2. Ibid., p. 51; Viswanatha, pp. 12–19; U. Ghoshal, *History of Indian Political Idea* (New York: Oxford University Press, 1959).

3. Ibid., p. 52.

were uniform. What "worked" for personal social behavior would "work" in domestic and international scenarios in this worldview.

THE HINDU LAW OF MAINTAINING INTERSTATE PEACE

Book VII of the Manu Smriti describes the duties of the king or *Raja-dharma*. A king must "try to triumph over his enemies by conciliation, corruption, or division, employed together or separately—never by warfare at the outset."[4] Kautilya's *Arthasastra* describes six initiatives of a king's foreign policy: peace by means of a treaty or *sandhi*, war or *vigraha*, neutrality or *asana*, alliance or *samsrya*, preparation for fighting or an expedition or *yana*, and peace with one ruler while at war with another ruler or *dvaidhibhavah*.[5] The usual peace treaty that bound the Hindu kings was the *sandhi*. The *sandhi* generally bound twelve kings into a network called a *mandala* or circle of states. Each *mandala* had a hypothetical ruler at its center called a *vijigsu*. The *vijigsu* was to rule by Dharma or the rule of righteousness. Because of his enemies or *ari*, five kings form the *vijigsu's* front and five his rear guard. One king would serve as the *vijigsus* ambassador or *madhyama*.[6] The *vijigsu* was to serve as an inter-sovereign peacekeeper by providing a balance of power of the states in the network. The wise *vjisgsu* was to serve as a *naphi* or center of gravity of the *mandala*.[7] The member states were to serve as *nemi* or spokes of the wheel.[8] If the *vijigsu* became oppressive to the states, Kautilya recommends that the states rise up against the *vijigsu* that "has risen for the destruction of all of us."[9] Kautilya also recommends that the *mandala* not commit acts of aggression against an ally or in violation of a treaty.

4. *Ibid.*, p. 52.
5. *Ibid.*, p. 52.
6. *Ibid.*, p. 52.
7. *Ibid.*, p. 53.
8. *Ibid.*
9. *Ibid.*, p. 52.

Such aggression places the *mandala* in unnecessary danger.[10] The ultimate goal for all the *vijigsus* was the unification of all *mandalas*. If one of the *vijigsus* could provide a superlative model for statecraft, the other *mandalas* could follow the example. If the model *vijigsu* continued his example, the other *vijigsus* would eventually join into one centralized kingdom. The centralized empire would replace the decentralized nation-states.[11] One worthy *vijigsu* who provided the superlative example necessary to unify all the nation-states would earn the title *chakravarti* or world emperor.[12] Like Confucianism, the ultimate goal of Hinduism was world unity in a context of universal morality.

The fundamental principle of contract law, *pacta sunt servanda*, receives treatment from Kautilya: "Pledging one's oath or hostage is of use only in this world, depending on strength. Thus kings of old, faithful to their word, made pacts by pledging their faith."[13] The principle of truth-telling and fulfillment of promises, articulated in the Hindu religio-political literature, is a near-universal religious principle.

THE HINDU LAW OF WAR

Hindu ideology holds war to be the alternative of last resort. Kings, according to Manu, should resort to war only after attempts at conciliation or *sama*, gift-giving or *dana*, and verbal expression of disagreement or *bheda*. Only after peaceful attempts should the king resort to the use of violent force or *danda*.[14] If a particular scenario provided equal advantages for both war and peace, the king should choose peace because war is inherently troublesome.

10. *Ibid.*, p. 52.
11. *Ibid.*, p. 53.
12. *Ibid.*, p. 53.
13. *Ibid.*, p. 53.
14. *Ibid.*, p. 54.

War causes a loss of wealth and increases evil in the world.[15] Vishwanatha similarly observes war as an option of last resort:

> Generally speaking, kings in ancient India did not engage in war unless they were forced to it; military expeditions were begun, not on sudden provocation or on small causes but only after great deliberation and on weighty issues. So at least declare the works on polity—*Arthasastras* and *Dharmasastras* alike.[16]

If war was inevitable, Hindu ideology holds that a declaration of war must precede hostilities. An enemy must be notified beforehand that a state of war exists. The declarations of war proceeded through envoys or *dutas*. These declarations were imperials writs or *sasanas* stating an ultimatum—submit to our terms or suffer a state of war.[17]

Once war begins, Kautilya describes three kinds of battles. The first kind of battle is the open battle. The open battle is fought during daylight and in specified regions. The second kind of battle is the treacherous battle. Treacherous battles are fought trapping, ambushing, and destroying a part of the enemy force. The third kind of battle is the silent battle. Silent battles were rather acts of espionage, including bribery.[18] In the Hindu military organization, the highest echelon consisted of a staff of thirty. The thirty, divided into six committees, had authority over the following six departments: admiralty, army service and transport, cavalry, chariots, and elephants.[19] *Arthasastra* meticulously described the functions of the various departments, the tactics of various battle formations, and rules regarding time and location of battle.[20]

---

15. *Ibid.*, p. 53.
16. *Ibid.*, p. 54; S. Vishwanatha, *International Law in Ancient India* 10 n. 1 (1929).
17. *Ibid.*, p. 54; Arthasastra, 2, p. 10.
18. *Ibid.*, p. 53; Arthasastra, 7, p. 3.
19. *Ibid.*, p. 55; S. Viswanatha, p. 140.
20. *Ibid.*, p. 55; S. Viswanatha, p. 150.

Ethical Limitations

All acts of war, however, must conform to the rule of righteousness, the Dharma Yuddha. The rules of righteousness in war required fairness.[21] Hindu armies must refrain from use of weapons that cause unnecessary pain and suffering. Concealed instruments, barbed weapons, poisoned projectiles, and burning projectiles were forbidden.[22] Further, a charioteer was forbidden to strike an infantryman. If a particular enemy solder is fighting with another comrade, the Hindu was forbidden to fight that enemy because he was already engaged. Hindu soldiers were also forbidden to strike non-combatants and combatants who surrendered.[23] The Greek envoy to the Mauryan Empire, Megasthenes, described the distinction between combatants and non-combatants. Because the Hindus regarded the farmer as a member of a "sacred and inviolable class," the Hindus would leave the farmers unmolested by the ravages of war.[24] Megasthenes also describes non-combatants as including onlookers who do not partake in the fight, those who are asleep, thirsty, fatigued, or those who are proficient artists.[25] Also, combatants whose armor had fallen off, a warrior who had laid down his weapon, and the mortally wounded were considered non-combatants. Hindu international law protected such non-combatants.[26] Combatants who were taken prisoner, including the wounded and sick, were to be treated humanely.[27]

Wanton and reckless destruction was also forbidden to the Hindu. Machines which caused wholesale destruction were forbidden to men of war because of the Hindu belief that military power could not be used except as necessary for victory, not total

---

21. *Ibid.*, p. 54; S. Viswanatha, p. 55.
22. *Ibid.*, p. 55; Manusmriti, 7, pp. 91–93.
23. *Ibid.*, p. 55; Manusmriti, 7, pp. 91–93.
24. *Ibid.*, p. 55; M. Bhatia, *International Law and Practice in Ancient India* (Delhi: Vikas Publishing House, 1977), pp. 100–101.
25. *Ibid.*, p. 55; Manusmriti, 7, pp. 91–93.
26. *Ibid.*, p. 55; Manusmriti, 7, pp. 91–93.
27. *Ibid.*, p. 56; S. Viswanatha, pp. 149–50.

destruction of natural resources.[28] Detailed rules regulated the treatment of conquered property.[29] Conquered peoples, including their manners and customs, must also be respected.[30]

THE HINDU LAW OF NEUTRALITY

According to Hindu ideology, a king could seek neutrality, or "self-imposed policy of nonintervention," if a state interest required it.[31] The *Mahabharata* offered several reasons why a king might seek neutrality: (1) If a king perceived that his state could not but be affected by a war, a king may establish a policy of nonintervention. (2) A king may seek neutrality if the war and its possible result would leave his state unaffected. (3) If a king knew that his involvement would tip the power balance in favor of one of the belligerents, a king may seek neutrality to avoid being identified as an enemy by the defeated party. (4) A king may realize that his state is virtually powerless to enter the war on either side and stand a high probability of victory.[32] According to Kautilya, there are three kinds of neutrality. First, a state may maintain neutrality by *sthana*, or keeping quiet. *Sthana* meant that a king maintained the status quo, i.e., other states maintained hostilities while he remained silent lest either side of the conflict take offense. Second, a state may maintain neutrality by *asana*, or withdrawing from hostilities because it is in the state's best interest to do so. Third, a state may maintain neutrality by *upekshana*, or by negligence in not taking measures against an aggressor.[33] Because Hindu doctrine regarded war as a last resort, a Hindu king would be inclined toward some kind of neutrality before the alternative of hostilities. Negotiations for neutrality were to precede war. Kautilya recommended that a

---

28. *Ibid.*, p. 55; S. Viswanatha, pp. 149–50.
29. *Ibid.*, p. 56; S. Viswanatha, pp. 154–55.
30. *Ibid.*, p. 56; Manusmriti, 7, p. 203.
31. *Ibid.*, p. 56.
32. *Ibid.*, p. 56; S. Viswanatha, pp. 154–55.
33. *Ibid.*, p. 57; Arthasastra, 6, p. 4.

king negotiate to the fullest degree in the *mantra-yudha* or battle of wits before the last resort of war.[34]

In the Hindu worldview, peace was preferred over war. The extremities of war produce greater opportunity for evil. The limitation of evil and the establishment of an environment for the greatest good is part of Hindu doctrine, and a principle of every major world religion.

---

34. *Ibid.*, p. 52; Arthasastra, 1, p. 16.

THE CHRISTIAN INFLUENCE ON THE DEVELOPMENT OF INTERNATIONAL LAW

THE FOUNDATIONAL CONTRIBUTION OF GROTIUS

Grotius' Purpose in Writing *De Jure Belli Ac Pacis*

Grotius has been described as the Christian "Father of International Law." Subsequent conservative Christian theologians have basically reiterated Grotius. In Grotius' preamble to *De Jure Belli Ac Pacis*, the first major Christian work devoted to the doctrine of international law, Grotius aimed at correction of nations' unnecessary resort to warfare in his day. In 1517, Martin Luther's Ninety-Five Theses began the sixteenth-century Protestant Reformation. The sixteenth century witnessed the establishment of rival mutually intolerant denominations of Christianity. Denominational intolerance motivated the bloody wars of religion that racked the seventeenth century. The ensuing loss of life was so colossal that Durant declaimed that the "carnage and desolation were probably greater than men had ever wrought in one generation in any land before."[1] Grotius witnessed the devastating Thirty Years' War from 1618 to 1648. The Peace of Westphalia in 1648 left Europe divided according to the religion of local princes. The

---

1. Mark W. Janis, "Religion and Literature in International Law," in *The Influence of Religion upon the Development of International Law* (Dordrecht: Martinus Nijhoff Publishers, 1991), p. 62; W. and A. Durant, *The Age of Reason* (New York: Simon and Schuster, 1961).

conflicts of religion became politically resolved. Grotius reflected upon the carnage in his preamble to *De Jure Belli Ac Pacis*:

> Throughout the Christian world I observed a lack of restraint in relation to war, such as even barbarous races should be ashamed of; I observed that men rush to arms for slight causes, or no cause at all, and that when arms have once been taken up there is no longer any respect for law, divine and human; it is as if, in accordance with a general decree, frenzy had openly been let loose for the committing of all crimes.[2]

Grotius witnessed the seemingly senseless bloodshed and asked "why?" As a seventeenth-century theologian of the Arminian Remonstrant school, Grotius sought religious solutions to international savagery. Grotius saw international butchery as a breach of both the Protestant and Catholic ethics.

But Grotius not only sought to terminate immoral wars between nations, he also sought "middle ground" in relation to the pacifists of his day, including the notable Erasmus. Erasmus and others of the pacifist persuasion held that no Christian should ever take up arms for any reason. Rather, the Christian should be like the harmless lamb and always respond to violence by turning the other cheek (*cf.* Mt. 5:38–42):[3]

> You have heard that it was said, "An eye for an eye and a tooth for a tooth." But I say unto to you, do not resist him who is evil; but whoever slaps you on your right cheek, turn to him the other also. And if anyone wants to sue you, and take your shirt, let him have your coat also. And whoever shall force you to go one mile, go with him two. Give to him who asks of you and do not turn away from him who wants to borrow from you.

To the pacifist perspective Grotius sought an answer, as his preamble states:

---

2. Janis, p. 62.

3. Matthew 5:38–42 according to the New American Standard Version (La Habra, C.A.: The Lockman Foundation, 1960).

THE CHRISTIAN INFLUENCE ON THE DEVELOPMENT

> Confronted with utter ruthlessness, may men, who are the very furthest from being bad men, have come to the point of forbidding all use of arms to the Christian, whose rule of conduct above everything else comprises the duty of loving all men. To this opinion sometimes John Ferus and my fellow-countryman Erasmus seem to incline, men who have the utmost devotion to peace in both Church and State.

Erasmus held Grotius' admiration because of his scholarship, but Grotius embarked upon writing theology that was biblically balanced. On the one extreme were the zealots who would seek the destruction of every other sect. Their causes would be colored by claims of divine vindication. Defenders of sectarian violence could cite, wrongly according to Grotius, texts of Scripture. Grotius declaims against such zealots as mere Christianized pragmatists:

> Such a work [as this][4] is all the more necessary because in our day, as in former times, there is no lack of men who view this branch of law with contempt as having no reality outside of an empty name. On the lips of men quite generally is the saying of Euphemus, which Thucydides quotes, that in the case of a king or imperial city nothing is unjust which is expedient. Of like implication is the statement that for those whom fortune favours might makes right, ad the administration of a state cannot be carried on without justice.[5]

On the other extreme, pacifists like Erasmus and Ferrus denounced the use of arms by citing, wrongly according to Grotius, texts such as Matthew 5:38–42. Describing his desired influence upon the pacifists, Grotius stated in his preamble:

> But their [the pacifists'][6] purpose, as I take it, is, when things have gone in one direction, to force them in the

---

4. Brackets' contents inserted by Janis, p. 63; Hugo Grotius, *De Jure Belli Ac Pacis Libri Tres* (Washington, D.C.: Carnegie Institution of Washington, 1925), Prolegomena, p. 9.

5. Janis, p. 63; Grotius, Prolegomena, p. 9.

6. Brackets' contents inserted for clarity.

opposite direction, as we are accustomed to do, that they may come back to a true middle ground. But the very effort of pressing too hard in the opposite direction is often so far from being helpful that it does harm, because in such arguments the detection of what is extreme is easy, and results in weakening the influence of other statements which are well within the bounds of truth. For both extremes therefore a remedy must be found, that men may not believe either that nothing is allowable, or that everything is.[7]

Grotius summarized the "middle ground" upon which sovereigns must stand in a good faith principle.[8] Sovereigns were given authority by God to make rules both domestic and international. However, sovereigns were required, according to the Christian religion, to keep their covenants with their own subjects and with other sovereigns. Grotius saw such good faith as an extension of the ninth commandment: "Thou shalt not bear false witness against thy neighbor." Even kings were not above God's moral law. In Grotius' chapter "On Promises," Grotius argues on the analogy that kings are like God. Because God keeps his promises, kings should also. Grotius' religious proofs abound in this chapter where Grotius argued that kings must be just. Since God is just, he keeps his promises. Since kings can not rule by injustice, kings must keep their promises. Grotius cites the Bible liberally on this argument, that the moral character of sovereigns should image the moral character of God:

> Nehemiah 9:8, "And thou didst find his heart faithful before thee. And didst make a covenant with him to give him the land of the Canaanite, of the Hittite, and the Amorite, of the Perizzite, the Jebusite, and the Girgashite—to give it to his descendants. And thou hast fulfilled thy promise, for thou art righteous."
>
> Hebrews 6:18, "In order that by two unchangeable things, in which it was impossible for God to lie, we might have

---

7. Janis, p. 62; Grotius, Prolegomena, p. 20.
8. Janis, p. 65.

strong encouragement, we who have fled for in laying hold of the hope set before us."

Hebrews 10:23, "Let us hold fast the profession of our faith without wavering, for he is faithful that promised."

First Corinthians 1:9, "God is faithful, through whom you were called into fellowship with his Son, Jesus Christ."

First Corinthians 10:13, "No temptation has overtaken you but such as is common to man; and God is faithful, who will not allow you to be tempted beyond what your able, but with the temptation will provide the way of escape also, that you may be able to endure it."

First Thessalonians 5:24, "Faithful is he who calls you, and He will also bring it to pass."

Second Thessalonians 3:3, "But the Lord is faithful, and He will strengthen and protect from the evil one."

Second Timothy 2:13, "If we are faithless, He remains faithful; for He cannot deny Himself."[10][9]

Sovereigns, therefore, are to be "faithful"—as good as their word. Grotius substantiates his argument regarding promises by arguing that promises are to be solemnized by oaths. Although Grotius states that oaths have always been of great force in most cultures, Grotius does not rely on custom as the authority by which kings should keep their oaths. Rather, Grotius cites again a divine analogy. Since God keeps his oaths, so should kings. Grotius uses a key text in Hebrews to underscore the inviolability of oaths: "Wherein God, willing more abundantly to show unto the heirs of promise the immutability of His counsel, confirmed it by an oath."[10] God's oath demonstrates God's commitment to keep his word; similarly, the oaths of kings should demonstrate their inviolable commitment to keep their word.

---

9. Janis, p. 64; Grotius, Book 2, Chapter 11, Section 4, p. 331.
10. Janis, p. 64; Grotius, Book 2, Chapter 13, Section 3, p. 365.

Grotius on International Relations between "Christian" and "Pagan" Nations

In another vein, Grotius treated a current issue regarding the proper subjects of international treaties. Some argued in the Reformation era that since some nations were pagan or Papist, truly Christian or "Reformed" nations should not enter into international treaties with them. Proponents of this view would cite texts which differentiate true believers from false believers. One key example of such a biblical text is Second Corinthians 6:14–18:

> Be ye not unequally yoked together with unbelievers. For what fellowship hath righteousness with unrighteousness, or what fellowship hath light with darkness? Or what concord hath the temple of the living God with idols? For are the temple of the living God, as God hath said, "I will dwell in them and walk among them and I will be a Father unto them and I will be their God and they shall be my people. Therefore, come out from among them and be ye separate, says the Lord, and touch not the unclean thing and I will welcome you, and I will be a Father unto you, and you shall be sons and daughters to me," says the Lord Almighty.

Grotius saw this text as applying ecclesiastically not internationally. True churches were to be separate from false churches. Further, true believers should not intermarry with those who are not. Grotius applied limits to this and other similar texts. Rather, he saw more specific texts relating to international relations as controlling whether nations of different Christian sects could form treaties and whether Christian and non-Christian nations could form treaties. Grotius held, citing a wide variety of both Old and New Testament texts, that nations could form international treaties despite differences in sect or religion. One key text that Grotius cites is Genesis 20. In this chapter Abraham, who was not only the patriarch of a family but the head of his own nation, formed a treaty with the pagan Abimelech. Each was to respect the watering rights of the others and agree to prevent any skirmishes between their servants regarding the shepherding of their cattle. Further, in

Genesis 18–19, Grotius cited how Abraham joined in a confederation of various pagan nations in order to rescue his captive nephew Lot. To Grotius, a king of a particular Christian sect could form an international treaty with a king of another Christian sect or even a non-Christian if the treaty was for a moral purpose and served the best interests of the king.[11]

---

11. Janis, p. 64; Grotius, Book 2, Chapter 14, Section 3, p. 382; Book 2, Chapter 15, Sections 1–3, pp. 391–2.

THE INFLUENCE OF ISLAM ON THE DEVELOPMENT OF INTERNATIONAL LAW

THE QURAN AS A SOURCE OF LAW AND GOVERNMENT

Quranic Law

The Quran is not only the Islamic holy book, it serves as a quasi-constitution and general source of law. The Quran is replete with law that applies both in the religious realm and the civil realm. The scope of its legal precepts includes the spiritual and the political.[1] For instance, Sura 7:47–48 establish a *lex talionis*, or standard of justice, for any court acting in the name of Islam to apply:

> It was We who revealed
> The Law (to Moses): therein
> Was guidance and light.
> By its standard have been judged
> The Jews, by the Prophets
> Who bowed (as in Islam)
> To God's Will, by the Rabbis
> And the Doctors of Law:
> For to them was entrusted
> the protection of God's Book,

---

1. For an example of commentary on the Quran, see generally Abu Ja'far Muhammad B. Jarir al-Tabari, *The Commentary on the Quran* (Oxford: Oxford University Press, 1978).

And they were witnesses thereto:
Therefore fear not men,
But fear Me, and sell not
My Signs for a miserable price.
If any do fail to judge
By (the light of) what God
Hath revealed, they are
(No better than) Unbelievers.

We ordained therein for them:
"Life for life, eye for eye,
Nose for nose, ear for ear,
Tooth for tooth, and wounds
Equal for equal." But if
Any one remits the retaliation
By way of charity, it is
An act of atonement for himself.
And if any fail to judge
By (the light of) what God
Hath revealed, they are
(No better than) wrong-doers.[2]

In the latter verse, the "eye for eye" standard is interpreted as a just retribution for any wrongdoing unless the wrongdoer undertakes some charity to atone for the wrongdoing.

The Quran's Doctrine of Government of Allah

The sovereignty of Allah is an all-inclusive concept in the Quran. Because Allah is sovereign, Muslims must obey or else be chastised by his hand. In a political sense, the "government of Allah" implies that the government of the Islamic nation does not belong to the people but to Allah. As Abdulla Yusuf Ali, a scholarly defender of Islam, argues:

> The concept of "sovereignty of God," in its turn, ensures political equality for all—the rulers and the ruled, and

---

2. Abdulla Yusuf Ali, *Translation of the Meanings of the Holy Quran* (Beirut: Khalil Al-Rawaf, 1961), pp. 256–58.

provides the basis for immunizing society from political tyranny. The sovereignty of God can be challenged only by atheists. But even in secular political philosophy, which projects the concept of the "sovereignty of the people," the term "people" stands for a corporation and a conceptual entity as it embraces the past, the present and the future generations of the people of the nation-state, bound all the time by the fundamental principle of a constitution established by the "founding fathers." Thus, there too, it is a "transcendental" entity in which sovereignty is affirmed. However, the antimony that emerges in affirming that the people are "sovereign" and "subject" at the same time created difficulties, which are avoided most rationally in affirming God a *sovereign* and the people as *subjects*.[3]

The Quran's Prescriptions on the Relation of Islamic Nations with Non-Islamic Nations

The Quran articulates strict prescriptions against association with "Christians" and "Jews." The Quranic strictures would include treaties with Christians and Jews. In the Quran 8:54–56, the Quran prohibits Muslims from making treaties with Christians and Jews, and promises "ruin" for those Muslims who do enter protective treaties with Christians and Jews:

> O ye who believe!
> Take not the Jews
> And the Christians
> For your friends and protectors:
> They are but friends and protectors
> To each other. And he
> Amongst you that turns to them
> (For friendship) is of them.
> Verily God guideth not

---

3. Muhammad Fazl-Ur-Rahman Ansari, *The Qur'ranic Foundations and Structure of Muslim Society* (Karachi: Indus Educational Foundation, n.d.), p. 193.

> A people unjust.
>
> Those in whose hearts
> Is a disease—thou seest
> How eagerly they run about
> Amongst them, saying:
> "We do fear lest a change
> Of fortune bring us disaster."
> Ah! perhaps God will give
> (Thee) victory, or a division
> According to His Will.
> Then will they repent
> Of the thoughts which they secretly
> Harboured in their hearts.
>
> And those who believe
> Will say: "Are these
> The Men who swore
> Their strongest oaths by God,
> That they were with you?"
> All that they do
> Will be in vain,
> And they will fall
> Into (nothing but) ruin.

Clearly, the Quran not only negatively prohibits "friendship" with Christians and Jews, it positively prescribes "friendship" with Muslims only. As the following text, 8:58–59, of the Quran states, "real friends" of the Muslim are only God and other Muslims:

> Your (real) friends are
> (No less than) God,
> His Apostle, and the (Fellowship
> Of) Believers,—those who
> Establish regular prayers
> And regular charity,
> And they bow
> Down humbly (in worship).
>
> And to those who turn
> (For friendship) to God,
> His Apostle, and the (Fellowship
> Of) Believers,—it is

The Fellowship of God
That must certainly triumph.[4]

The Quranic Doctrine of "Mosque" and "State"

To the Quran, there is no separation between the religious body and the political body. There is no line of distinction: the two are one entity. At the inception of Islam, the prophet was both spiritual leader and military leader. There was never a distinction between religious and political realms:

> Islam thus evolved differently from Judaism and Christianity, the other monotheistic faiths which existed in Arabia and the surrounding lands and which were mentioned many times in the divine relations. ... In the case of Islam, religion was the state—with its Prophet acting as the military commander, making war and peace, collecting taxes, laying down the law and dispensing justice. In contrast, Christ made a distinction between what belonged to God and what belonged to Caesar at the very outset. Since Christianity has recognized two separate authorities—Church and State—existing sometimes in harmony and sometimes in conflict ...

Judaism, however, does not maintain as strict a distinction between its religious organization and its political organization. Bu there is, however, a prophet/priest distinction in the Hebrew Scriptures. Further, in the Hebrew Scriptures, the king could not perform priestly duties, and any who tried, like Saul, Israel's first king, were divinely punished. As the Islamic scholar Hiro remarks:

> As for Judaism, the situation is unclear: classical rabbinical Judaism emerged only after the Hebrew state had ceased to exist. Judaism, therefore, falls uneasily between Islam and Christianity as far as relations between the state and religion are concerned.[5]

---

4. Ali, p. 261.

5. Dilip Hiro, *Holy Wars: The Rise of Islamic Fundamentalism* (New York: Routledge, 1989), p. 9.

THE INFLUENCE OF ISLAM ON THE DEVELOPMENT

The Constitution of Medina is an enlightening example of the Quranic relation between religious and political realms. In A.D. 627, this epic constitution laid the foundation for the Islamic *umma* and the *Dar al Islam*, the Realm of Islam. The Constitution of Medina first established a solid united Islamic community composed of believers and their dependents, the *umma*. The *umma* was subdivided into clans or subdivisions which were individually responsible for blood money and ransoms. The members of the *umma* must show solidarity against crime. *Umma* members were not allowed to give respite to a criminal even if the criminal was a near kinsman. Further, both in war and peace, the Muslims composing the *umma* must maintain solidarity. In case of a dispute between the *umma* members, the dispute would be settled by Allah and Muhammad.[6] The solidarity of the *umma* is maintained by the five pillars of Islam. The pillars of Islam are a matrix of individual and social obligations: *shadith* (saying), *shahada* (act of religious witness), *salat* (prayer), *sakat* (purification), and *sawm* (the annual fast of Ramadon with the *hajr*, the holy flight or pilgrimage to Mecca).[7]

Increasing Secularization under the Realities of Statecraft over Conquered Peoples

The Muslim state began as an aspiring theocracy, with a worldview that all nations should be converted to Islam either by persuasion or by the sword and that all nations would be ruled by the Quran. However, the realities of international politics produced an increasing secularization of the Muslim adherents. After the death of Muhammad, his surviving cousin and nephew were supplanted by a Mu'awiya, who took the reins of the Muslim state. Mu'awiya was far more realistic than the religiously idealistic Muhammad and his cousin and nephew. Mu'awiya introduced the art of Byzantine statecraft using a judicial structure similar to the Byzantine model.

---

6. Ali, p. 8.
7. Ali, p. 10.

As cunning, intrigue, and corruption began to infect the courts of the Muslim cleric-judges, the theocratic worldview gave way to the painful and mundane realities of maintaining power over conquered peoples. Islam began to absorb the Persian wisdom of statecraft through the apt Arab pupils of Persian viziers. A Persian convert to Islam, Ibn al-Muqaffa', was a secretary in the court of both the Omayyads and the first of the Abbasids of Persia prior to their fall to Islam, and translated into Arabic the Persian Pahlavi, the royal chronicles and court manuals of Sassanian Iran.[8]

Islamic Poetry—A Reflection of the Islamic View of International Relations

An old adage, "poets are the unofficial legislators of mankind," implies that the minds of men and women are more ruled by the pen than they are by the sword. The following excerpts from Islamic poetry reveal the passionate cry of the beating heart of Islam against internal corruption and external political domination. The following poem calls out for revolt against the rule of infidel nations:

> Of the hireling's blood outpoured
> Lustrous rubies makes the lord;
> Tyrant squire to swell his wealth
> Desolates the peasant's filth.
> Revolt, I cry!
> Revolt, defy!
> Revolt, or die!
>
> City sheikh with string of beads
> Many a faithful heart misleads,
> Brahman baffles with his thread
> Many a simple Hindu head.
> Revolt, I cry!
> Revolt, defy!
> Revolt, or die!

---

8. Arthur J. Arberry, *Aspects of Islamic Civilization as Depicted in the Original Texts* (London: George Allen and Unwin, Ltd., 1964), pp. 14–15.

THE INFLUENCE OF ISLAM ON THE DEVELOPMENT

Prince and Sultan gambling go;
Loaded are the dice they throw—
Subjects soul from body strip
While their subjects are asleep.
Revolt, I cry!
Revolt, defy!
Revolt, or die!

Brother Muslims, woe to us
For the havoc science does!
Ahriman is cheap enough,
God is rare scarce-offered stuff.
Revolt, I cry!
Revolt, defy!
Revolt, or die![9]

Mohaad Iqbal, who died ten years before the realization of his vision of an independent Islamic nation composed of the Indian provinces now called Pakistan, wrote the following call to rebellion to his fellow Muslims in northern India:

Little flower fast asleep,
Rise narcissus-like, and peep;
Lo, the bower droops and dies
Wasted by cold griefs; arise!
Now that birdsong fills the air
And muzzins call to prayer,
Listen to the burning sighs
Of the passionate hearts, and rise!
　Out of leaden sleep,
　Out of slumber deep
　　Arise!
　Out of slumber deep
　　Arise!

Now the sun, that doth adorn
With his rays the brow of morn,
Doth suffuse the cheeks thereof

---

9. The work of Muhammad Iqbal, who after his death was hailed as the Muslim prophet of Pakistan. Iqbal inspired fellow Muslims in India to revolt in order to effect Muslim reforms. Independent Muslim nationhood was, according to Iqbal, the only means to the end of Indian oppression. *Ibid.*, pp. 379–80.

With the crimson blush of love,
Over mountain, over plain
Caravans take route again;
Bright and world-beholding eyes,
Gaze upon the world, and rise!
    Out of leaden sleep,
    Out of slumber deep
      Arise!
    Out of slumber deep
      Arise!

All the Orient doth lie
like strewn dust the roadway by,
Or a still and hushed lament
And a wasted sigh and spent,
Yet each atom of this earth
Is a gaze of tortured birth:
Under India's and Persia's skies,
Through Arabia's plains, O rise!
    Out of leaden sleep,
    Out of slumber deep
      Arise!
    Out of slumber deep
      Arise!

See, thy ocean is at rest,
Slumbrous as a desert waste;
Yea, no waxing or increase
E'er disturbs thy ocean's peace.
Ne'er thy ocean knoweth storm
Or Leviathan's dead swarm:
Rend the breast and billow-wise
Swelling into tumult, rise!
    Out of leaden sleep,
    Out of slumber deep
      Arise!
    Out of slumber deep
      Arise!

Listen to this subtlety
that reveals all mystery:
Empire is the body's dust,

Spirit true Religion's trust:
Body lives and spirit lives
By the life their union gives,
Lance in hand, and sword at thighs,
Cloaked, and with thy prayer mat, rise!
    Out of leaden sleep,
    Out of slumber deep
      Arise!
    Out of slumber deep
      Arise!

Thou art Pure and worshipful
Guardian of eternal Rule,
Thou the left hand and the right
Of the World-possessor's might.
Shackled slave of earthy race,
Thou art Time, and thou art Space:
Wine of faith that fear defies
Drink, and from doubt's prison rise!
    Out of leaden sleep
    Out of slumber deep
      Arise!
    Out of slumber deep
      Arise!

Against Europe I protest
And the attraction of the West:
Woe for Europe and her charm,
Swift to capture and disarm!
Europe's hordes with flame and fire
Desolate the world entire;
Architect of Sanctuaries,
Earth awaits rebuilding; rise!
    Out of leaden sleep,
    Out of slumber deep
      Arise!
    Out of slumber deep
      Arise![10]

    The Islamic Republic of Pakistan is a direct result of a national revolt inspired by the vision of an Islamic international order.

10. *Ibid.*, pp. 379–81.

Iqbal, like his Islamic fellow revolutionaries before him since the eighth century, dreamed of a "world united in glad acceptance of the challenge of Islam, the challenge to man and men to make themselves sharers with God in the creation of a perfect and perfectly self-realizing Universe."[11]

The Islamic Doctrine of Holy War or J'had

Islamic law has a violent and militarily aggressive dimension. At least 78 times the Quran refers to Holy War or J'had.[12] The Holy War is an incremental part of Islamic international political thought. For an Islamic nation to commit a wanton act of aggression against an infidel nation may be appear immoral by Western moral and political standards, but the Quran condones, even commends, such aggression. The Quran promises divine assistance to those Muslims who endeavor national conversion by means of force (3:11, 111–12, 122–26; 8:9–12, 17, 42–44, 126; 9:25–27; 35:25, 27).[13] War and religion are combined in the passages on J'had.

But to enjoy Allah's assistance in battle, the Islamic army must submit to Allah's regulations and rules of J'had (4:71, 94, 104; 5:33–34). Islamic warriors were to pray constantly for victory (4:101–03). The Quran serves to inspire Muslims to fight against infidels. Muslims are roused and encouraged for Holy War in a wide variety of passages (2:19–97, 216, 244; 3:120–27, 138, 164–167, 194; 4:35, 74–77, 84; 8:39–40, 46, 59, 60, 65–66; 9:29). Further, the Quran excoriates any Muslim who through cowardice shrinks back from going into battle (4:75, 95; 9:38, 43, 83; 33:13–20). The historical sections of the Quran include at least 242 verses on the various battles of Muhammad (Ahzab or Khandaq, 33:9–25; Badar, 3:13, 123–24, 163–67; Badar-e-Sughra, 5:83–84; Bani Mustalaq, 63:1–8; Bani Saleem, 100:1–5; Khaiber, 48:27;

---

11. *Ibid.*, p. 381.

12. *Subject-Wise Index to the English Koran* (Karachi: Peermahomed Ebrahim Trust, 1973).

13. *Ibid.*, p. 63.

THE INFLUENCE OF ISLAM ON THE DEVELOPMENT

Hunain, 9:25–27; Tabuk, 9:38–123; Uhud, 3:121–22, 125–129, 139–40, 164–79; Destruction of Bani Quraizah, 33:26–27; Exile of bani Nuzeer, 59:2–6; Sirreyyah of Abdullah Bin Jahash, 2:217; Hudaibyyah and Bait-e-Rezwan, 48:4, 18; forecast of Victory of Mecca, 48:27).[14] The Quran produces an aggressive nationalist fortress mentality, viewing the gains of Islam as non-negotiable and what is not Islam as a target for military aggression.

The Nebulous Nature of Islamic Political Thought

Islamic political thought is not a well-defined complex of propositions. Rather, Islamic political thought is composed of "generalities, broad statements of goals and a vague conception of a constitutive process."[15] The general formulation of pure Islamic theory, as espoused by the resurgent fundamentalists, is simple theocracy. God's will is superior to everyone else's. The will of the majority is irrelevant if that will contradicts the divine will. A rule of the people, by the people, and for the people, is therefore foreign to a pure Islamic government. Since the divine will is the crux of the Islamic political theory, those who have devoted their entire lives to finding God and knowing his mind are those who have the right to rule.[16] The model Islamic state is one ruled by the religious clerics according to the Quran. Lawyer-clerics are Allah's mouthpiece to the Islamic community, communicating the all-important will of Allah.

The Development of an Islamic Orthodoxy

When Islam began its career of conquest, it had "no theology and very little law so that within wide limits every man did that which

---

14. *Ibid.*, pp. 22–23.
15. M.H.A. Reisman, "Islamic Fundamentalism and Its Impact on International Law and Politics," in *The Influence of Religion upon the Development of International Law* (Dordrecht: Martinus Nijhoff Publishers, 1991), p. 116.
16. *Ibid.*, p. 117.

was right in his own eyes."[17] During the first three centuries of Islam, the body of orthodox Islamic opinion divided into two categories, each with its own adherents.[18] The Sunni held that Quran and the body of commentary surrounding it and the life of Muhammad were the final and complete revelations of Allah. Therefore, no Muslim cleric could add to that revelation from Allah. The Shia branch held that specially inspired imams, or prophets, could be raised up by Allah to communicate Allah's will to his people. These prophets could not contradict the Quran, but could add to it by providing specific guidance to Allah's people.

Islamic Law and International Law

The Islamic fundamentalism is a core ideology that grows in the number of its adherents. This ideology tends to oppose Westernization and revisionism of historic Islamic ideology and tradition. The growth of Islamic fundamentalism is a major phenomenon. As Ismail Seragedlin, a modern scholar of Arab studies, notes:

> The Arab world today is in the throes of a major, though subtle, upheaval. Everywhere, in every Arab country, a rekindling of interest in religion and religious affairs is noticeable. In some cases this takes the form of the resurgence of militant political Islamic fundamentalism. In other cases, it takes the form of overt zealotry and adherence to patterns of ritual, dress, and behavior associated with medieval Muslim societies, even when many of these patterns of behavior contain little if anything that is inherently Islamic. Examples of this behavior would be growing of beards (inspired by prophetic lore), the wearing of certain clothes among women, and even the refusal of some of the more fervent young zealots to sleep on beds.[19]

17. A.S. Tritton, *Muslim Theology* (Bristol: Luzac and Company, Ltd.: 1947), p. 9.

18. *Ibid.*

19. Ali E. Hillal Dessouki, *Islamic Resurgence in the Arab World* (New York: Praeger Publishers, 1982), p. 54.

Actually, the Prophet Muhammad predicted, "At the turn of each century there will arise in my nation a man who will call for a religious revival."[20] The goal of the Islamic fundamentalist resurgence is the conversion of *anomie*. Anomie is that state in which "normative standards of conduct and belief are weak or lacking and is commonly characterized by disorientation, anxiety, and isolation."[21] The standard to which each state must conform in order to overcome *anomie* is the Divine Law in the Quran. The Divine Law is not provincial and limited to Muslims only. All nations are subject to the Islamic law. Therefore, when Islamic fundamentalists call for imposition of the Divine Law, the very imposition has inherent international implications. The teleology of Islam, like the teleology of Marxist-Leninism, is universal conformity to their ideological strictures. Accordingly, national conversion to Islam, whether more extreme Shiite fundamentalism or more moderate Sunni, is viewed as another beachhead to advance upon the entire globe.[22]

The Practical Problems of Imposition of Islamic Law upon Nations

The traditional Western safeguards of human liberty eclipse into insignificance in the face of Islamic legal reformation.[23] Those who would impose the Islamic Divine Law see that law as superhuman. The kind of regime the Islamic proponents desire is "too good for most human beings."[24] Butterworth, the Islamic authority from the University of Maryland, sees the Divine Law standard like the

---

20. Dessouki, Introduction.

21. Dessouki, p. 55.

22. "Lecture on Teaching and Learning," in *An Islamic Response to Imperialism: Political and Religious Writings of Sayyid Jamal Al-Din "al-Afghani,"* trans. Nikki R. Keddie (Berkeley: University of California Press, 1968), pp. 101–05, 107.

23. Charles E. Butterworth, "Prudence Versus Legitimacy," in *Islamic Resurgence in the Arab World*, (New York: Praeger Publishers, 1982), p. 109.

24. *Ibid.*, p. 110.

political morality espoused by Socrates' speech on the model city in Plato's *Republic*. Socrates saw the moral standards of his model city as practically unattainable in the here and now.[25] However, those standards espoused by Socrates for the model state were to be goals and ideals to which the developing state, however laden with human imperfections, must strive.

Principles, of course, are necessary for any social order; but the practical means of imposing such principles are the only criteria by which any society can determine the expedience of any particular proposal for reform. Principles in the non-phenomenal realm are of little use in solving the complex issues facing any society unless those principles can put on shoe leather, touch the ground, and direct a society toward betterment. For instance, the social principle of *Ijmac,* or agreement between citizens, rings true in virtually any society, whether theistic, atheistic, or pluralistic.[26] The principle, simply stated, is that a society should take on no initiative, to use Lyndon Johnson's oft repeated pat phrase, unless "there appears to be a consensus." Such a principle rings true from even common logic. As Jesus stated, "A kingdom divided against itself cannot stand." Lenin repeated the obverse of the principle when he predicted the division of the West, and its division and devouring by the Eastern bloc. But, how is one to implement the principle? Should democracies therefore be as pure as possible, where every contingency is placed to a referendum, as far as administrative burdens will allow? Or, does *Ijmac* require only that referenda be held only in the form of free elections? On what issues should elected officials turn to popular referenda, or are opinion polls the best fulfillment of the *Ijmac* requirement? As long as such principles remain non-phenomenal with no procedural dimension, such principles will do little good outside a merely academic environment. The Islamic principles, however idealistically noble, must have a concrete procedural dimension in order to be valuable

---

25. Plato, *Republic*, trans. Paul Shorey (Cambridge, Mass.: Harvard University Press, 1963), pp. 500ff.

26. Butterworth, p. 110.

realistically. At some point, ideas, in order to useful, must become practical.

Methodological Considerations in Evaluating the Ramifications of Islamic Resurgence to International Law

The phenomenon of the Islamic resurgence has received increasing attention from socio-historical academia, the media, and the governments threatened by such resurgence. The Islamic resurgence seeks replacement of Western imported legal systems with Quran-based social mores, statutes, and judiciaries. Various terms, including "revivalism," "revitalization," "upsurge," reassertion," "renewal," "awakening," "fundamentalism," "neofundamentalism," "resurgence," "militant Islam," and "political Islam," have described the new phenomenon. The increasing activism in the name of Islam demands analysis. Often however, an analysis of such activism degenerates into sensationalism. The media, in its ever-urgent quest for captivating news, finds a "the Muslims are coming!" attitude enticing. Images of the Islamic hordes laying siege to Vienna conjure greater interest by the media's clientele.[27] *Newsweek*, for instance, referred to the resurgence as "Islam on the march."[28]

Another tendency in the attention the Islamic resurgence receives by the Western media is retrogression. Often the Islamic resurgence is viewed as a reaction to the inevitable evolution of societies away from a religious orientation. The new dogmatism is viewed as a reaction to the toleration of divergent secular views fostered by modernity. The new political resolve is viewed as religious extremism. Religious revivalism is considered an anachronism in a scientific age. To reviews of the Islamic resurgence with such an aura, religion and sociology are separate disciplines and the designation of social issues such as the rights of women

---

27. Ali E. Hillal Dessouki, "The Islamic Resurgence: Sources, Dynamics, and Implications," in *Islamic Resurgence in the Arab World*, (New York: Praeger Publishers, 1982), p. 4-5.

28. *Newsweek*, December 5, 1977, pp. 58-59.

and the freedom of (secular) expression as religious ones is out of whack.[29]

Yet other treatments of the contemporary Islamic resurgence exhibit actual denial of the nature of the resurgence. One aspect of the denial is that all forms of the resurgence are rigidly uniform. Admittedly, the various elements of the resurgence agree in that the Islamic Divine Law or *sharica* should be applied universally. However, elements of the resurgence differ in attitude, social context, self-definition, political allegiance and activism, and immediate objectives. Further, adherents of the new resurgence may themselves deny a "newness" at all to the resurgence. Adherents claim that the "new" resurgence is merely the numerical and spiritual growth of the old historic Islam.[30] The resurgence, to them, is not new but rather an expansion of what was already there in embryonic form.

SPHERES OF ISLAMIC POLITICAL ACTIVISM

The Eradication of Western-Imported Legal Systems and the Reinstitution of Islamic Law

Islamic political activism manifests in six particular categories. First, in the legal realm, Islamic activists move to eradicate Western-imported legal systems and reinstitute Islamic law. More pronounced expressions of the movement away from generally accepted Western legal standards include the penal amputations according to the Divine Law or *sharica* in Libya and Mauritania and public flogging of malefactors in Abu Dhabi.[31] In 1971, Egypt included *sharica* as a source for constitutional and legislative law.

---

29. Similarly, irreligious elements in the Western press may disdain any form of Christian resurgence evidenced in the 1980, 1984, 1988, and even 1992 U.S. presidential elections and the pro-life movement. Johannes Fabian, "The Anthropological of Religious Movements from Explanation to Interpretation," *Social Research* 46 (1979), 4ff.; James Fernandez, "On the Notion of Religious Movement," *Social Research* 46 (1979), 36ff.

30. Dessouki, p. 5.

31. *Ibid.*, p. 10.

Eight years later the *sharica* was made the sole source for legislation.³² Three years later the Egyptian parliament passed legislation forbidding any Muslim from imbibing beverage alcohol publicly. Further, the law forbad the sale of beverage alcohol in public areas other than those zones specifically designated as tourist zones. In 1978, Mauritania determined that *sharica* should be applied to all its domains and that pre-existing legislation must be revised accordingly. The purpose of such legislative reform was to reaffirm Mauritania's "original identity."³³ Sudan established a government committee to examine options to amend their constitution to conform to *sharica* in 1978.³⁴

Increased Religious Allusion and Symbolism

A second sphere of manifestation of Islamic political activism is religious allusion and symbolism. In Egypt for instance, Sadat was generally known as the "believing president" or *al-ra'is al-mu'min*. Almost all of Sadat's speeches concluded with a religious allusion or quotation. Further, to boost his political agenda, Sadat often referred to his opposition as unbelievers, especially if they were socialistic leftists. *Anathema* became a key "buzz" word to label his political opponents. The 1973 war against Israel was code named Badr, a key battle of the Prophet Muhammad. Previously, Nassar in Egypt received forceful criticism from Jordan, Saudi Arabia, and Yemen for importing "atheistic" socialism in 1961–64. In 1975, North Yemen established a watchdog department, the first its kind, to monitor the "imported ideologies which oppose Islamic teachings and traditions."³⁵ Even the ancillary influence of the tourist trade became a target of "Islamization" in Kuwait. In 1978, Kuwait imposed strict restrictions on dancing shows in hotels and

---

32. Dessouki, p. 11.

33. *Arab Report and Record*, June 16–30, 1978, p. 444.

34. Andrew Lycett, "The Great Islamic Revival," in *Arabia and the Gulf*, No. 21 (May 28, 1979), pp. 8–9.

35. *Arab Report and Record*, August 1–15, 1975, p. 530.

nightclubs. The name of art could be used to cloak anti-Islamic practices that "violate the Islamic structure of Kuwait."[36]

Further, more moderate Arab leaders reflected more sensitivity to the changing religious scene by paying more attention to strengthening Islamic sentiment. The most secular of Arab leaders, Bourguiba, started to throw sops to the Islamic right by appeasing and cooperating with their political spokespersons. Bourguiba even gave speeches in the pulpits of the two most influential mosques, Zaytuna and Qayrawan.[37] Mohammar Qahdhafi propagates a unique brand of Islam to bolster his political power base.[38]

Metamorphosis of Social Mores

A third sphere of manifestation of rising Islamic sentiment is the realm of social mores. An increasing number of young men wear their beards in traditional Islamic manner. An increasing number of educated younger women wear modest apparel in a way that has been uncommon for decades. The traditional women's apparel leaves only the face and hands uncovered.[39] Surveys conducted in Tunisia in 1967 and 1973 revealed a definite increase in personal religious practices, including the observance of total abstinence from beverage alcohol. Abstainers increased from 46 percent to 73 percent and attendance at religious events increased from 18 percent to 61 percent.[40]

---

36. *Arabia and the Gulf*, no. 46 (November 13, 1978), p. 5.
37. Dessouki, p. 11.
38. Ibid., p. 11.
39. Dessouki, pp. 11–12.
40. M.A. Tessler, "Political Change and the Islamic Revival in Tunisia," *Maghreb Review* 5 (1980), pp. 14–15.

THE INFLUENCE OF ISLAM ON THE DEVELOPMENT
Political Activist Organizations

The fourth sphere of manifestation of Islamic activism is the increase of political opposition organizations. In Egypt for example, four militant Islamic organizations have emerged. The Muslim Brothers Association circulates a monthly magazine called *al-Dacwa* or "call." This periodical draws heavy criticism from the Egyptian government. Three underground militant groups also appear on the Egyptian political horizon. *Jamacat al-Takfir wa'l-Hijra* or Repentance and Holy Flight, *Shabab Muhammad* or Muhammad's Youth, and *Jund Allah* or God's Soldiers are currently alive and well as underground sociopolitical dissenting groups.[41]

Further, the Islamic resurgence has borne fruit on university campuses. Student organizations known as *al-Jamaca al-Islamiya* or the Islamic Association exist at every university. By the late 1970s the *al-Jamaca al-Islamiya* had become the "strongest and cohesive political force on Egyptian campuses."[42] These student groups cry out for the application of *sharica*. Most of the demonstrations against the Shah's residence in Egypt were instigated and manned by religious students. The agitation of the student dissent reached such proportions in May of 1980 that Sadat ordered all student religious societies disbanded. The ban instituted by Sadat was justified as a remedy to "religious fanaticism, extremism, and communal strife."[43]

Some Islamic dissenters have congregated around Muslim preachers. The two most charismatic mosque preachers are Sheikh Muhammed al-Ghazali and Sheikh Kishk. Thousands would flock to hear the Friday Khutbas of these dynamic preachers. Eventually, the former was removed from his post. The latter's sermons are taped and sold commercially in bulk. His appeal is largely emotional and borders on the sensational.[44]

---

41. Dessouki, p. 12.
42. Dessouki, p. 12.
43. Dessouki, p. 12.
44. Dessouki, p. 12.

In Algeria, Tunisia, the Gaza Strip, and Sudan, Islamic activism has surfaced in force. The Tunisian government responded with both restrictive and conciliatory actions. Government spokesmen in Tunisia accused Islamic activists of "reviving fanaticism and obscurantism."[45] For three months in 1979, the Tunisian government banned the activist Islamic *al-Mujtmac* or Society. To conciliate the activists, however, the Tunisian government restricted the hours of public beverage alcohol consumption in 1980. Further, the government revoked licenses to bars in the capital. In Algeria, public demonstration by Islamic activists included the public humiliation of El-Oued prostitutes, liquor stores ransacked in rioting, and in Algiers, the capital, and Oran demonstrators demanding reform in education.[46] Peaceful demonstrations occurred in Ouargla, Biskra, and Touggourt.[47] In 1980, Palestinian activists burned liquor stores, movie theaters, and other businesses providing entertainment.[48] In Sudan, the 300-member National Assembly included 60 representatives who were Muslim Brothers.[49]

International Organizations to Promote Unity among Islamic Nations

The fifth sphere of manifestation of Islamic activism is the proliferation of international organizations to promote political and economic relations between Islamic states.[50] Pan-Islamic sentiment

45. Patrick Blum, "Islamic Revival Fuels Maghreb Discontent," *Middle East Economic Digest* 23 (November 1979), pp. 5–7.
46. *Middle East Newsletter* 130 (December 7, 1979–January 13, 1980), pp. 10–11.
47. *Middle East Newsletter* 130 (January 28–February 10, 1980), p 4.
48. Dessouki, p. 13.
49. Dessouki, p. 13.
50. For a discussion of Quranic banking, prohibitions on usury, and legitimate profit, see generally Nabil A. Saleh, *Unlawful Gain and Legitimate Profit in Islamic Law* (Cambridge: Cambridge University Press, 1986). Iran, for instance, has established two Quranic state-supported banks that offer loans without interest.

fuels several organizations that seek to foster stronger political and economic ties, even political union, between Islamic states. Some of these organizations seek union of all Arabs into a pan-Arabic state united by ethnic, cultural, and religious commonality. Other organizations seek union of all Islamic nations, including Pakistan, Indonesia, and Turkey into a colossal Islamic state bound in religious solidarity.[51]

Educational Reform

A sixth sphere of manifestation of Islamic activism is education. In 1977, the first international conference on Islamic education was held in Saudi Arabia.[52] 40 countries participated and approved an initiative to adopt "an education policy that is based on Islamic outlook and that derives its principles from Islamic sources."[53] The conference focused specifically on the methodology of teaching the sciences. Islam sees any gap between religions and science as purely artificial. The conference therefore recommended a plan to "close the artificial gap between religion and science which was imported along with European methodology."[54] Consequently, both Tunisia and Algeria reformed their public school curricula to increase Islamic studies.[55]

THE DELICATE BALANCE MODERATE ARAB STATES MUST FOLLOW IN FOREIGN POLICY

The following quotation from the Arab scholar Dessouki demonstrates the tightrope upon which the ruling family of Saudi Arabian kingdom must walk balancing international relations and domestic policy:

51. Dessouki, p. 13.
52. *Arabia and the Gulf*, no. 21 (May 22, 1978), p. 9.
53. *Ibid.*
54. *Ibid.*
55. Dessouki, p. 12.

The Saudi ruling class faces a difficult choice. To the extent that it keeps the symbols of the traditional bases of legitimacy—tribe and religion—alive, the more it remains vulnerable to the challenge o Islamic orthodoxy. If, on the other hand, it moves to establish a new basis of legitimacy, it will be eroding its own position and privileges. Here lies the dilemma: the royal family cannot keep the traditional structure of social and political relations unchanged, nor is it ready to accept the eventual consequences of social change, particularly those related to political participation. A delicate balance was established in the 1960s by King Faial and was made more effective in the 1970s by the oil wealth. But the divergence between a rapidly changing society and its political structure remains.[56]

A FOCUS ON SHIITE ACTIVISM

The Shiite branch of the Islamic world has taken the posture of the shock troopers for Allah. Demonstrations, assassination attempts, and political maneuvers have evidenced the resurgence of this branch of Islam and its consequent disdain of imported Western ideology, business, and culture. The Shiite community in Saudi Arabia numbers at least 250,000 and is largely domiciled in the oil-rich eastern province. Demonstrations increase, especially in response to the Saudi link with the United States, the supporter of Israel. On the Ashura feast day in 1980, for instance, riots erupted during the celebration of the martyrdom of al-Husayn ibn Ali in November 1979.[57] In Iraq, Shiite demonstrations turned violent as early as 1977 in the holy cities of Najaf and Karbala. The Mujahidin, a militant Shiite group, claimed responsibility for the failed assassination attempt on Tariq Aziz, the most senior Christian in the Iraqi government. Saddam Hussein reacted with the immediate execution of Ayatollah Baqir al-Sadr, the ranking Shiite figure

---

56. Dessouki, p. 16.

57. *Middle East Newsletter* 130 (December 7, 1979–January 13, 1980), pp. 7–8.

in Iraq. In Kuwait, for instance, the government deported the personal representative of the Ayatollah Khomeini, Hojatollislam Abba al-Muhri, his son, and their associates, even though some were Kuwaiti citizens. In November 1979 Kuwaiti Shiites marched on the U.S. embassy but were dispersed by tear gas.[58] In Lebanon, Imam Musa al-Sadr founded the "movement of the deprived," a Shiite activist organization which includes a military unit, *amal* or "hope."[59]

A FOCUS ON THE ROLE OF ISLAMIC RESURGENCE IN THE FOREIGN POLICY OF QADHDAFI

After the 1969 revolution where Qadhdafi came to power, a systematic program of institutional *sharica* was inaugurated. Qadhdafi's vision of the ideal Islamic state is the *Jamahiriya*, a state where Muslim masses rule themselves according to the *sharica*. The particular tenets of his vision for the perfect theocratic Islamic society are articulated in his *Green Book*, the ideological treatise of his brand of Islam.[60]

The General Pattern of Erosion of *Sharica* and Absorption of Western Legal Codes

An increasing phenomenon in Libya as well as the entire Arab world is the establishment of a Western educated elite. This elite generally includes a large number of lawyers and business professionals. As Mayer, professor at the Wharton School, remarks:

> Persons educated along European lines increasingly came to dominate legislative and judicial activities and, as lawyers, formed an influential, new professional class.

---

58. *Economist*, December 13, 1980.

59. Dessouki, p. 13.

60. Ann Elizabeth Mayer, "Islamic Resurgence or New Prophethood: The Role of Islam in Qadhdafi's Ideology," in *Islamic Resurgence in the Arab World* (New York: Praeger Publishers, 1982), p. 196.

So consistent was the progress of this Westernization of the law that it came to seem inexorable. Although Muslim clerics and other traditionally minded Muslims objected to the abandonment of the *sharica* and even formed movements like the Muslim Brethren to campaign for its revival, the Westernized elites who ran the legal systems in Muslim countries remained indifferent to their concerns.[61]

There are two areas of law, however, not only in Libya but the whole Muslim world, that are so strongly imbedded in Libyan society that even the Western-influenced elite dare not touch—Quranic family and inheritance law.[62] According to the Quran, spouses own equal shares of marital property. The legal system prior to Qadhdafi's takeover was similar to the French model, and thus was similar to the system in Egypt, Syria, and Iraq. After Qadhdafi's successful revolution, a commission was established to examine current Libyan law and recommend steps to reform the legal system according to the *sharica*. The most significant contribution of this commission was the reform of penal sanctions. The existing criminal code contrary to the *sharica* was revoked and the five crimes in the Quran for which there is a criminal penalty, the *hadd*, were instituted. The criminal penalties include 100 lashes for fornication, 80 lashes for slanderous imputation of unchastity, 40 lashes for consumption of beverage alcohol, amputation of the hand for theft, and amputation of the hand and foot for brigandage. A minor change to the then-existing legal system based on the *sharica* was the provision for the state to collect part of the alms tax, the *zakat*.[63]

---

61. Mayer, p. 197.

62. *Ibid.*, p. 197.

63. Muammar Qadhdafi, *The Green Book. Part One: The Solution of the Problem of Democracy* (London: Martin Brian and O'Keefe, 1976), p. 31.

THE INFLUENCE OF ISLAM ON THE DEVELOPMENT

Qadhdafi's Role of Limiting the *Sharica* in Libya

Qadhdafi's reforms, however, are not completely consistent with *sharica*. First, Qadhdafi abolished separate jurisdiction of the *sharica* courts, leaving all jurisdiction to secular courts. Second, the Islamic tradition of leaving a family *waqf*, a trust fund set up to provide designated beneficiaries with income, was also abolished. Third, the *sharica* in domestic law was set aside by setting minimum ages for marriage, eliminating forced marriages, a reduction of an ex-husband's alimony if he could demonstrate the ex-wife was at fault, and allowing the wife the option of divorce if she could pay a court-determined indemnification to her husband.[64]

Qadhdafi's Redefinition of the Divine Law, the *Sharica*

Qadhdafi's *Green Book* contains three parts. The first part, the *sharicat al-mujtama*, literally "law of society," outlines Qadhdafi's view of the basis of his new society. The orthodox Muslim, according to *sharicat* theory, believes that Allah is the sole legislator who deposits his sacred law (*sharica muqaddasa*) in the Quran and the *sunna*, or the customs of the Prophet Muhammad. Under classical *sharica* theory, the *sharica* exists in rigid form with no possibility for new legislation. The majority Sunni position is that the *sharica* can not be amended, altered, or modified. The *sharica* exists solely to govern as it is and the sole function of government is to provide a court implement whereby the *sharica* can be applied. The *Shiite* theory differs in that the *Shiites* believe that divinely inspired imams in their religious capacities can make new laws.

Qadhdafi, therefore, in "good politician" style, claimed the rigid application of *sharica* theory while at the same time excluded a major part of it. In part two of Qadhdafi's *Green Book*, Qadhdafi redefined the *sharica* as containing solely the Quran, not the Sunna of the Prophet Muhammad and the vast corpus of commentary on the *sharica* contained in the *fiqh*, the vast body of recorded medieval jurisprudence. In 1977, Libya adopted a new constitution

64. *Ibid.*, p. 198.

establishing the authority of the Allah as sovereign and the people as subjects, but Allah's law as exposited by *Green Book*, and the people's rights and responsibilities as exposited by the *Green Book*.

Qadhdafi's Attack on Islamic Shirk or Para-Quranic Religious Documents

In one of Qadhdafi's speeches in 1978 he further articulated his unique doctrine of *sharica*. He stated that the Prophet Muhammad was merely a vehicle for revelation according to Sura 46:9. Therefore, Muslims should look solely to the Quran for their religious authority rather than the Sunna of the Prophet. Further, Qadhdafi argued that the Quran, unlike the Bible, was accurately recorded.[65] Qadhdafi assailed Christianity's Holy Book, contending the text of the Bible was not an accurate contemporaneous record, having been redacted by numerous later editors who merely recorded inflated hearsay that passed from generation to generation. According to Qadhdafi, mischievous compilers had adulterated the Bible with unsubstantiated alterations.[66] Faulty oral traditions incorporated into the Bible Qadhdafi called *shirk*. But Muslims should not follow *shirk* either; the Prophet's traditions were subject to *shirk* as much as the alleged oral traditions of the Christians.

In the same speech Qadhdafi assailed the role of imams and clerics. Because the Quran was written in clear and understandable Arabic, no intermediary should come between the Quran and the Muslim. The Muslim should not regard imams as divine spokesmen. To Qadhdafi, the Quran alone is the mouthpiece of Allah. No one should ascend the *minbar*, the mosque's pulpit, to tell Muslims what they should believe. Islamic scholars were not an essential part of any Muslim's religion. Qadhdafi specifically attacked any para-Quranic writings as unnecessary to the full understanding of the Islamic faith. At a festival on July 3, 1978, at the largest mosque in

---

65. Muammar al-Qadhdafi, *al Sijill al-qawmi, bayanat wa kutab wa ahadith al-aqid Muaccmar al-Qadhdafi* (Tripoli: Mathaat al-Thawra al-arabiy, 1978), pp. 466–83, as cited by Mayer, p. 201.

66. Mayer, p. 201.

THE INFLUENCE OF ISLAM ON THE DEVELOPMENT

Tripoli Qadhdafi "preached" the same doctrine of "sola Quran."[67] At the mosque the local cleric, the *ulama*, was in the congregation. The *ulama* and Qadhdafi argued over the validity of the *hadith*, the written reports about the Prophet's Muhammad's actions. Qadhdafi argued that the *hadith* was entirely unreliable historically and therefore no Muslim should hold the *hadith* as a source of religious authority. The *ulama* countered, holding that study of the *hadith* was a science that enabled the Muslim scholar to determine what were reliable reports about the Prophet and what reports were not authentic. Although both Qadhdafi and the *ulama* agreed that there was a consensus, an *ijma*, that certain standard collections of the *hadith* were trustworthy, Qadhdafi nonetheless held that Muslims had no definite revelation from Allah or proof that false *hadith* had been inserted into even these standard collections. Qadhdafi substantiated his claim by citing the historical milieu of the formulation of the *hadith*, where antecedents of the Sunni and Shiite branches of Islam fought over succession. Qadhdafi further substantiated his claim by citing self-contradictions in the *hadith* and between the *hadith* and the Quran.[68]

Qadhdafi's Standing with Shiite Revolutionaries

Although Qadhdafi was a fierce Arab nationalist, Shiites hardly regard him as persona grata. Qadhdafi's modification of the *sharica*, his attacks on the *hadith*, his denials of the *ulama*, his denial of the authority of imams, clerics, and scholars cause the Shiite activists to cringe. To the Shiites, Qadhdafi was heterodox and should be either "instructed" or removed.[69] Qadhdafi established his own

67. Qadhdafi here remarkably resembles the great Christian reformer, Martin Luther, in this doctrine. Luther held that although Christian scholars were helpful in determining the meaning of Scripture, they were not essential to understanding Scripture. On religious authority, Luther held the sole source of authority was the Bible, not the Church's clerics. To Luther, the issue in faith and practice was not what does the church say the Scripture says but what does the Scripture say?

68. Qadhdafi, pp. 997–1009 as cited by Mayer p. 202.

69. Mayer, p. 218.

unique Islamic theology where he alone became the preeminent prophet-lawgiver to the exclusion of any Muslim cleric. In the judicial sphere, Qadhdafi's own appointed secular judges composed the judiciary (the *sharica* religious courts he abolished). In the political sphere, Qahdhafi's opponents had a marked predilection to disappearance. In the religious sphere, Qadhdafi's *Green Book* and the Quran are the sole written authoritative sources of Islamic religion.

A FOCUS ON THE IRANIAN REVOLUTION AND ITS DOCTRINE OF INTERNATIONAL EXPANSION

Islam as a Catalyst for International Revolution

The Ayatollah Khomeini was not trained as a politician, neither as a diplomat, but rather as a theological teacher. Because of his fierce attacks on monarchy, he was exiled by the Shah of Iran. Khomeini, however, made great use of annual pilgrimages to Mecca. At such festivals, he decried monarchy as a form of government that was anti-Quranic and condemned Iran becoming an American vassal state. In 1977, the Democratic Presidential candidate, Jimmy Carter, called for a better human-rights record from America's allies. His call spurred the Shah to release over three hundred political prisoners. These prisoners included some of the Islamic intelligentsia—lawyers, politicians, and Islamic clerics. More and more, at the orchestration of Khomeini, various sectors of society took to the streets in demonstrations. Khomeini, who himself was Shiite, addressed the Iranian military, which was largely Shiite. He told the Iranian war machine that those who shoot at their fellow Muslims are shooting at the Quran. With the overthrow of the Shah, Khomeini returned to a national assembly of 2 million at Tehran which demanded as Islamic state. Later, a national referendum consisted of a single question: "Should Iran become an Islamic Republic?" Every Iranian had an identity card which would be stamped "yes" should they vote yes. Therefore, out of fear of being labeled an infidel, over 89 percent of the populace voted in the national referendum. Of those who voted, over 90 percent voted "yes," thus having their identity cards stamped "yes." At that point, Khomeini declared the beginning of the "Government of Allah."[70]

The mosque had become the vestibule of a new religious order in Iran. At the mosques Khomeini had established revolutionary committees to orchestrate the revolution in Iran. Khomeini's Friday sermons at the *minbar* became the chief inspiration for revolt. International revolution against monarchy and the establishment of Islamic republics became the religious international call. Therefore, the Shia branch of Islam became a synonym for international religious revolution. Shia was infused with a new militancy by *imams* such Khomeini who were deemed as new inspired prophets of Allah to lead the *Dar al Islam*, the Realm of Islam, from the darkness of infidelity to national Quranic observance.

The International Ramifications of the Rise of Ayatollah Khomeini

The rise of the Ayatollah Khomeini's institution of *Valiat-Faghih* in Iran illustrates an implementation of Islamic theocracy.[71] The domestic structure of the Iranian theocracy also reflects the theocratic principle. Under Article 91, a council of twelve individuals appointed by the "maximum leader," the Ayatollah, oversees the Iranian Parliament to confirm that each of its resolutions are consistent with Islamic principles. Six of the council are Muslim clerics appointed by the *Valiat-Faghih*. The other six are Muslim lawyers chosen by the Parliament. Under Article 93, the Parliament's authority is null and void without the sanction of the council of twelve. In event of deadlock in the council of twelve, the supremacy of the clerics is established by Article 96. Article 3 (16) of the Iranian constitution articulates the foreign policy of Iran. All foreign relations must be "based on Islamic principles,

---

70. Dilip Hiro, *Holy Wars: The Rise of Islamic Fundamentalism* (New York: Routledge, 1989), pp. 164–169.

71. Reisman, p. 118; Ayatollah Ruhollah Khomeini, *Islamic Government* (Arlington, V.A.: Joint Publications Research Service, 1979), p. 105.

brotherly commitment towards all Muslims and the complete support for the oppressed peoples of the world."[72] Therefore, the interstate relations of the Iranian theocracy are merely an extension of the theocratic principle.

Militant Shia Fueling War with Iraq

With Khomeini's grip on power firm in Iran, he began to denounce secularist such as the Baathist Party in Iraq, including the Baathist president Hussein. Hussein, from the outset of the Iranian Revolution, had been receiving reports of low morale in the Iranian military and general societal undercurrents decrying the new religious despotism. With non-Shiites populating the oil-rich province on the Iraq-Iran border, Hussein ordered his forces to "liberate" this province. The Iraqi forces however were stalemated.

But the Iraqi attack on Iran caused the Iranian Islamic revolution to move from its anti-American phase, as evidenced by the taking of the American embassy and its hostages, into a patently anti-secularized Arab phase. Khomeini, from the early days in the war with Iraq, denounced Saddam Hussein as a "pagan." Khomeini stated that since Hussein had attacked the Iranian Islamic Republic after its self-declaration as a "Government of Allah," Hussein had actually attacked Allah and those who serve him according to the Quran. Therefore, true Muslims should see the war with Iraq as a *jihad* or holy war with infidels.[73]

National Statutes Resulting from the Shiite Revolution

The Shiite Revolution in Iran established a new order predicated on various Articles drafted by the Islamic Parliament. Those who drafted the constitution conceded to demands of the primarily Sunni Kurds, Baluchs, and Arabs for tolerance of Islamic sects other than Shiite. Article 12 of the Iranian constitution states:

72. Reisman, p. 121.
73. Hiro, pp 180–184.

THE INFLUENCE OF ISLAM ON THE DEVELOPMENT

The official religion of Iran is Islam and the Twelver Jaafari school of thought, and this principle shall remain eternally immutable. Other Islamic schools of thought, including the Hanafi, Shafii, Maliki, Hanbali, and Zaidi schools, are to be accorded full respect, and their followers are free to act in accordance with their own jurisprudence in performing their religious devotions. These schools enjoy official status for the purpose of religious education and matters of personal status (marriage, divorce, inheritance and bequests), being accepts in the courts relating to such matters.

Article 5 of the constitution states because of the death of Hazrat Vali Asr or Lord of the Age, the missing Twelfth Imam,

> The governance and leadership of the nation devolve upon the just and pious *faqih* who is acquainted with the circumstances of his age; courageous, resourceful and possessed of administrative ability; and recognized and accepted as Leader by the majority of the people.[74]

The replacement of the twelfth imam is described in Article 1 as the "Grand Ayatollah Imam Khomeini." A replacement for the Ayatollah will be according to Article 107:

> Whenever a candidate who has outstanding characteristics for leadership is found, he will be introduced to the people as the Leader. Otherwise, three or five candidates who fulfill the conditions for leadership will be appointed members of the Leadership Council and introduced to the people.[75]

The leader must be fully conversant with "the issues of the day and circumstances of his age."[76]

Although the constitution outlines the place for a "maximum leader," the first chapter of the constitution describes the application of the basic Quranic principle of community. Chapter one establishes a multi-tiered system of government. The multi-tiered

---

74. Hiro, pp. 172–73.
75. Hiro, p. 173.
76. Hiro, p. 175.

system issues from the Quranic texts 42:38, "their affairs are by consultation among them," and 3:153, "consult them on affairs." The Iranian constitution lays out three branches, executive, legislative, and judicial. The judicial branch, according to a descending order of appellate relation, includes Supreme Judicial Council, a Provincial Council, Municipal Council, and City, Neighborhood, Division, Village Council.

The rights of the citizens of the Islamic Republic of Iran are delineated by the new constitution. The judiciary, according to Article 156, has the function of "restoring public rights and promoting justice and legitimate freedoms."[77] Chapter Three of the constitution contains twenty-three articles. Article 21 includes the rights of women according to "Islamic criteria." Article 24 states what are the rights of the press: "Publications and the press are free to present all matters except those that are detrimental to the fundamentals of Islam or the rights of the public. Article 26 also states the right to political parties: "the formation of political and professional parties, associations and societies, as well as religious societies, whether they be Islamic or pertain to one of the recognized religious communities is freely permitted on the condition that they do not violate the principles of independence, freedom, national unity, the criteria of Islam or the basis of the Islamic Republic." Article 26 goes further to state: "No one may be prevented from participating in the above groups, or be compelled to participate in them."[78]

Article 49 delineates the right to property, subject to government limitations:

> The government has the responsibility of confiscating all wealth resulting from usury, usurpation, bribery, embezzlement, theft, gambling, misuse of endowments, misuse of government contracts and transactions, the sale of uncultivated lands and other categories of land

---

77. Hiro, p. 175.
78. Hiro, p. 176–77.

inherently subject to public ownership, the operations of houses of ill-repute, and other illegal sources.[79]

Article 49 further outlines the property rights under the Iranian Republic:

> When appropriate, such wealth must be restored to its legitimate owner, and if no such owner can be identified it must be placed in the public treasury. The application of this principle must be accompanied by investigation and verification in accordance with the law of Islam and carried out by the government.[80]

Article 35 describes the jurisprudential rights of the citizen of the Islamic Republic. In any dispute, "both parties to a dispute have the right in all courts of law to select a lawyer." Article 35 states "if they are unable to do so, arrangements must be made to provide them with legal counsel."[81] Further, Article 38 forbids the use of torture, and adds that the punishment of those who violate the ban "will be determined by law." Article 25 provides for privacy rights for Iranian citizens. The following is forbidden:

> Inspections of letters and the failure to deliver them, the recording and disclosure of telephone conversations, the disclosure of telegraphic and telex communications, or the willful failure to deliver them, wiretapping and all forms of covert investigation.[82]

Although the rights delineated may please the Western ear, reports continue to pour in from Iran regarding the torture of prisoners. Further, no political parties have formed.

---

79. Hiro, p. 176.
80. Hiro, p. 176.
81. Hiro, p. 176.
82. Hiro, p. 176.

THE IMPACT OF THE CONSTITUTION OF THE ISLAMIC REPUBLIC UPON INTERNATIONAL LAW

The Pan-Islamic Component of the Iranian Constitution

The Iranian Constitution is definitively pan-Islamic according to Article 10: "This your nation is a single nation." As Article 10 states:

> The government of the Islamic Republic of Iran has the duty of formulating its general policies with a view to the merging and union of all Muslim peoples, and it must constantly strive to bring about political, economic and cultural unity of the Islamic world.[83]

Article 152 is more specific, stating that the Islamic Republic's foreign policy includes the "defense of the rights of all Muslims" and the "non-alignment with respect to the hegemonist superpowers."[84] Article 154 "sanctifies" the export of revolution as the religious duty of Iranian citizens:

> The Islamic Republic of Iran considers the attainment of independence, freedom and just government to the right of all peoples in the world. It therefore protects the just struggles of the oppressed and deprived in every corner of the globe.

Khomeini declared that the "Islamic duty" of its citizens was to support national liberation movements of the "deprived peoples" of the world. Khomeini's foreign minister, Ibrahim Yazdi, stated regarding oppressed peoples in 1979, that the Khomeini regime "only wanted [them] to benefit from Iran's experience and gain strength from Iran's support."[85] Khomeini stated that "if the revolution kept within Iranian borders, it would become vulnerable."[86]

Therefore, the export of Shiite revolution is not only desirable to the new Iranian regime, it is part and parcel of their domestic

---

83. Hiro, p. 207.
84. Hiro, p. 207.
85. Hiro, p. 207–8.
86. Hiro, p. 208.

law. Religion and state eclipse in the Iranian constitution, causing both law and religion to serve the single end of converting all of Islam, and later the entire world, to the republican form of Shiite government, i.e., the "government of Allah." The establishment of a worldwide fellowship of Islamic republics is the end of the Iranian constitution.

INTERNATIONAL RESPONSE TO THE IRANIAN REVOLUTION

The Formation of the Gulf Cooperation Council

In response to the open statements of the Iranian constitution regarding the export, including armed export, of Shiite revolution caused the various surrounding Arab states, especially those with large populations of Shiites, to fear for their present existence. Since the Iranian revolution claims to be republican, the democratic aura of the Iranian revolution may appeal to the politically voiceless masses of the various modern feudal monarchies—Kuwait, Saudi Arabia, Qatar, the United Arab Emirates, and Oman. Because of fear of internal disorder, if not outright revolt, Kuwait, Saudi Arabia, Qatar, the United Arab Emirates, and Oman formed the Gulf Cooperation Council. This supra-national body would even call upon the help of the West "for military assistance in case of serious threat to one or more of its members."[87] The goals of the Gulf Cooperation Council are to "co-ordinate internal security, procurement of arms and the national economies of the six member states."[88]

Specific responses of the member nations to the Iranian revolution have been fierce. The Bahraini prime minister stated, for instance, "The Iranian regime is instigating the Shias in Bahrain and the Gulf under the slogans of the Islamic revolution ... training them in the use of weapons and acts of sabotage and sending

---

87. Hiro, p. 210.
88. Hiro, p. 210.

them to their countries to foment chaos and destroy security."[89] The Saudi interior minister Prince Nayif offered to send Saudi troops to Bahrain to prevent a coup. According to Nayif, "the sabotage plot was engineered by the Iranian government and was directed against Saudi Arabia." As a result of Iranian expansionism, the Gulf leaders drew together to maintain their authoritative regimes. They will not let loose of their monopoly on political power easily.[90]

The militant Shiite vision of a "government of Allah" over all nations will not be realized without massive bloodshed even among the other conservative Arab states. The union of the Arab world around Shiite revolutionary goals will not occur with just the dire opposite of the peaceful harmony the Quranic concept of *umma* requires. Worldwide international Islamic utopia appears a great way off.

---

89. Hiro, p. 211.
90. Hiro, p. 211.

CONCLUSION

In sum, religious worldviews have principles which apply to the international arena. A common ground between the religious philosophic systems surveyed is the common morality and happiness of all mankind. Worldwide peace, harmony, and order, or the Confucian *ping*, provides a common teleology for the religious worldviews. Each religion presupposes justice is the indispensable stepping stone to happiness. Universal morality is the principle at which these major world religions intersect; would that such worldwide utopian harmony could be a bit closer to reality.

BIBLIOGRAPHY

Sayyid Jamal Al-Din "Lecture on Teaching and Learning," in *An Islamic Response to Imperialism: Political and Religious Writings of Sayyid Jamal Al-Din "al-Afghani,"* trans. Nikki R. Keddie. Berkeley: University of California Press, 1968.

Ali, Abdulla Yusuf. *Translation of the Meanings of the Holy Quran.* Beirut: Khalil Al-Rawaf, 1961.

Ansari, Muhammad Fazl-Ur-Rahman. *The Qur'ranic Foundations and Structure of Muslim Society.* Karachi: Indus Educational Foundation, n.d.

Arabia and the Gulf, No. 21 (May 22, 1978), p. 9.

Arabia and the Gulf, No. 46 (November 13, 1978).

Arberry, Arthur J. *Aspects of Islamic Civilization as Depicted in the Original Texts.* London: George Allen and Unwin, Ltd., 1964.

Bhatia, M. *International Law and Practice in Ancient India.* Delhi: Vikas Publishing House, 1977.

Blum, Patrick. "Islamic Revival Fuels Maghreb Discontent." *Middle East Economic Digest* 23 (November 1979), pp. 5–7.

Butterworth, Charles E. "Prudence Versus Legitimacy," in *Islamic Resurgence in the Arab World.* New York: Praeger Publishers, 1982.

Chen, L.F. *The Confucian Way: A New and Systematic Study of the Four Books.* 1977.

Confucius, *Great Learning.* China: Commercial Press, 1923.

Dessouki, Ali E. Hillal. *Islamic Resurgence in the Arab World* New York: Praeger Publishers, 1982.

Durant, W. and A. *The Age of Reason.* New York: Simon and Schuster, 1961.

Fabian, Johannes. "The Anthropological of Religious Movements from Explanation to Interpretation." *Social Research* 46 (1979), pp. 4ff.

Fernandez, James. "On the Notion of Religious Movement." *Social Research* 46 (1979), pp. 36ff.

Economist, December 13, 1980.

Ghoshal, U. *History of Indian Political Idea.* New York: Oxford University Press, 1959.

BIBLIOGRAPHY

Hugo Grotius, *De Jure Belli Ac Pacis Libri Tres* Washington, D.C.: Carnegie Institution of Washington, 1925.

Hiro, Dilip. *Holy Wars: The Rise of Islamic Fundamentalism.* New York: Routledge, 1989.

Janis, Mark W, ed. "Religion and Literature in International Law," in *The Influence of Religion on the Development of International Law.* Dordrecht: Martinus Nijhoff Publishers, 1991.

Khomeini, Ayatollah Ruhollah. *Islamic Government.* Arlington, Va. Joint Publications Research Service, 1979.

Legge, James. *The Chinese Classics.* Delhi: Motilal Banarsidass, 1966.

Lloyd, Lord of Hampstead. *Introduction to Jurisprudence.* London: Stevens, 1979.

Lycett, Andrew. "The Great Islamic Revival," in *Arabia and the Gulf*, No. 21. May 28, 1979.

"Political Change and the Islamic Revival in Tunisia," *Maghreb Review* 5 (1980), pp. 14–15.

Mayer, Ann Elizabeth. "Islamic Resurgence or New Prophethood: The Role of Islam in Qadhdafi's Ideology," in *Islamic Resurgence in the Arab World.* New York: Praeger Publishers, 1982.

Middle East Newsletter 130. December 7, 1979–January 13, 1980, pp. 10–11.

Middle East Newsletter 130. January 28–February 10, 1980, pp. 4.

Middle East Newsletter 130. December 7, 1979–January 13, 1980, pp. 7–8.

Moses, Jeffry. *Oneness: Great Principles Shared by All Religions.* New York: Fawcett Columbine, 1989.

New American Standard Version. La Habra, C. A.: The Lockman Foundation, 1960.

Plato. *Republic.* trans. Paul Shorey. Cambridge, Mass.: Harvard University Press, 1963.

Qadhdafi, Muammar. *The Green Book. Part One: The Solution of the Problem of Democracy.* London: Martin Brian and O'Keefe, 1976.

al-Qadhdafi, Muammar. *Al Sijill al-qawmi, bayanat wa kutab wa ahadith al-aqid Muaccmar al-Qadhdafi.* Tripoli: Mathaat al-Thawra al-arabiy, 1978.

Reisman, M.H.A. "Islamic Fundamentalism and Its Impact on International Law and Politics," in *The Influence of Religion upon the Development of International Law.* Dordrecht: Martinus Nijhoff Publishers, 1991.

Subject-Wise Index to the English Koran. Karachi: Peermahomed Ebrahim Trust, 1973.

Tessler, M.A. *Arab Report and Record*, August 1–15, 1975.

Tritton, A.S. *Muslim Theology.* Bristol: Luzac and Company, Ltd., 1947.

Viswanatha, S. International Law in Ancient India 10, 1929.[1]

---

1. Gatgounis, G. (2014). *International Law Afloat on a Sea of World Religions.* Charleston, SC: George J. Gatgounis.

www.ingramcontent.com/pod-product-compliance
Lightning Source LLC
Chambersburg PA
CBHW070059100426
42743CB00012B/2592